●═ EVALUATING EMPLOYEE PERFORMANCE

A Practical Guide To Assessing Performance

Paul J. Jerome

Richard Chang Associates, Inc.
Publications Division
Irvine, California

EVALUATING EMPLOYEE PERFORMANCE

A Practical Guide To Assessing Performance

Paul J. Jerome

Library of Congress Catalog Card Number
97-66178

ISBN 1-883553-62-8

Richard Chang Associates, Inc.
Publications Division
15265 Alton Parkway, Suite 300
Irvine, CA 92618
(800) 756-8096 • Fax (714) 727-7007
E-Mail: info@rca4results.com

ACKNOWLEDGMENTS

About The Author

Paul J. Jerome is Vice President of Richard Chang Associates, Inc., a diversified organizational improvement consulting and publishing firm based in Irvine, California. He is an experienced management consultant and business executive specializing in executive development, management training, team building, and performance management. Paul is widely recognized for his creative design and enthusiastic delivery of practical management tools and techniques. He is also the author of *Coaching Through Effective Feedback* and *Re-Creating Teams During Transitions*, published by Richard Chang Associates, Inc.

Paul would like to acknowledge the support of the entire team of professionals at Richard Chang Associates, Inc. for their contribution to the guidebook development process. In addition, special thanks are extended to the many client organizations who have helped us shape the practical ideas and proven methods shared in this guidebook.

Additional Credits

Editors: Doug Dalziel and Ruth Stingley

Reviewers: Shirley Codrey and Susan Parker

Graphic Layout: Dena Putnam and Christina Slater

Cover Design: Eric Strand and John Odam Design Associates

PREFACE

The 1990's have already presented individuals and organizations with some very difficult challenges to face and overcome. So who will have the advantage as we move toward the year 2000 and beyond?

The advantage will belong to those with a commitment to continuous learning. Whether on an individual basis or as an entire organization, one key ingredient to building a continuous learning environment is *The Practical Guidebook Collection* brought to you by the Publications Division of Richard Chang Associates, Inc.

After understanding the future *"learning needs"* expressed by our clients and other potential customers, we are pleased to publish *The Practical Guidebook Collection*. These guidebooks are designed to provide you with proven, *"real-world"* tips, tools, and techniques— on a wide range of subjects—that you can apply in the workplace and/or on a personal level immediately.

Once you've had a chance to benefit from *The Practical Guidebook Collection*, please share your feedback with us. We've included a brief *Evaluation and Feedback Form* at the end of the guidebook that you can fax to us at (714) 727-7007.

With your feedback, we can continuously improve the resources we are providing through the Publications Division of Richard Chang Associates, Inc.

Wishing you successful reading,

Richard Y. Chang
President and CEO
Richard Chang Associates, Inc.

TABLE OF CONTENTS

What we hope we never hear in discussions regarding our performance:

"Thank you for meeting my low expectations."

"It's not my fault! It's the stupid form. Anyway, signing it doesn't mean you have to agree."

"I really don't remember much about your performance except that fiasco you were responsible for last month."

CHAPTER ONE

INTRODUCTION

Chances are, you've been in the role of an evaluator. It might have been when you were evaluating the performance of your team members, the merits of a new employment opportunity, or the talent on your child's sports team. Likewise, you've also probably been evaluated. Most organizations insist on it, whether it's called a performance evaluation, appraisal, or review.

Picture this: your manager is in a long black robe, sitting behind a huge desk. You, on the other hand are sitting in a rather small chair facing your accuser. It's judgment day, and you are about to receive the dreaded performance evaluation. Leaning back in the chair and with arms folded, your manager says, *"I've carefully considered your performance and can see you have a long way to go."*

If this is how you picture a performance evaluation, you're not alone. Successful people from all walks of life cringe at the prospect of a work evaluation, and it doesn't really matter whether you're on the giving or receiving end. Most people feel uncomfortable when they have to sit in judgment of other people, and would prefer not to be judged by others.

Unfortunately, these feelings about performance evaluations become self-fulfilling. When you don't expect good things to come of them, you often get what you expect. Wasn't it Mark Twain who said, *"Like porcupines in love, appraisals are a pain for both parties"?* Well, he must have had a special type of experience—bad!

For those of you who hold this opinion of performance evaluations, there's some good news. It doesn't have to be like this. The cycle of discomfort can be broken. Performance evaluations can be used effectively to recognize, reward, develop, redirect, and document the performance of people who work with you. And it can be done painlessly, through good planning and involvement with your team members.

"This hurts me far more than it hurts you."

Why Read This Guidebook?

If you look forward to performance evaluations with the same enthusiasm you have for an Internal Revenue Service audit, this guidebook is for you. If you've ever had a boss judge you according to a laundry list of *"personality traits"* that had little to do with your job, this guidebook is also for you.

On the other hand, maybe you've found performance evaluations to be helpful to all parties—maybe you even genuinely enjoy the process. *(You may be "different," but others still love you...)* This guidebook is still for you, because it will provide insights into how to instill this value in others and maintain high morale during the appraisal process. You can even pass this practical reference on to others and make their lives *(and yours)* that much easier!

At the very least, *Evaluating Employee Performance* will provide you with techniques that will help you get through the evaluation process more effectively and efficiently. And, as a bonus, you may even change your mind about *"just how bad it is!"* Before you know it, you may even look forward to performance evaluations *(really!)*, because they provide an opportunity to recognize contributions, encourage development, and work together to improve performance.

Who Should Read This Guidebook?

Evaluating Employee Performance will help everyone who is in an organizational position that requires the documentation of individual and team performance—including his or her own performance. Whether it's an annual performance evaluation for a direct report, or much more frequent progress reports to advise upper management about business activities, the time-tested techniques found in this guidebook will prove invaluable. And they can be applied to a variety of organizations and industries.

It matters little that your organization is service-related or a manufacturing environment, or whether you work for a profit or a non-profit organization. Since performance evaluations are almost universally applied, why not take the initiative to make them better? It's better than the alternative.

When And How To Use It

Use this practical guidebook as a resource before, during, and after performance evaluations. It's designed as an *"easy read."* You can finish it in a few hours. Maybe you should even give one as a gift to someone who really needs it *(like your boss!)*.

If it's your job to evaluate the members of your department, staff, or team, and you want to make your job a little easier to digest, find the time to read this guidebook. It definitely won't hurt. And maybe, just maybe, you'll move evaluating employee performance from the *"don't want to do"* to the *"don't mind doing"* category.

Note: Throughout this guidebook, *"work group"* and *"team"* will be used interchangeably to mean the staff members of your organization, department, division, committee, or task force. The people on your staff are defined as *"team members,"* which is also the same as employees, associates, group members, contractors, consultants, suppliers, etc. Likewise, managers and supervisors sometimes are referred to as *"team leaders."*

THE BIG PICTURE

Evaluating performance is not an event. It's a process that includes up-front planning and regular maintenance. It requires time. It demands thought. And it begins way before you start writing or typing on a performance-evaluation form. Sitting down for a half hour the day before your employee is scheduled for a performance evaluation just won't cut it.

The Performance Management Cycle

Performance evaluation is only one part of the continuous cycle that managers can use to manage individual and team performance. Yes, believe it or not, ending up with effective performance evaluations means you have to start at the beginning with the Planning Phase.

PERFORMANCE MANAGEMENT CYCLE

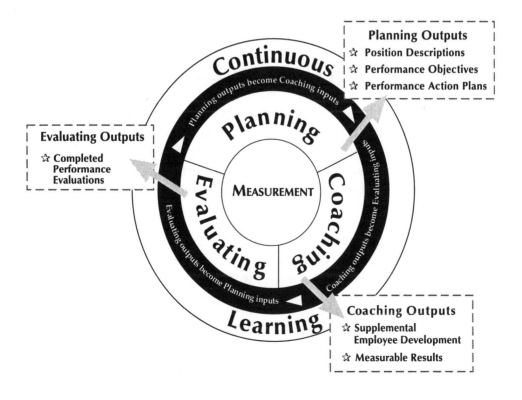

During the Planning Phase, you and your employee jointly develop a performance plan. The performance plan acts as a road map for the Performance Management Cycle, and impacts both the Coaching and Evaluating Phases. *(These two topics are covered in detail in the practical guidebooks, **Planning Successful Employee Performance** and **Coaching For Peak Employee Performance**, published by Richard Chang Associates, Inc.)*

There are three components of an employee performance plan:

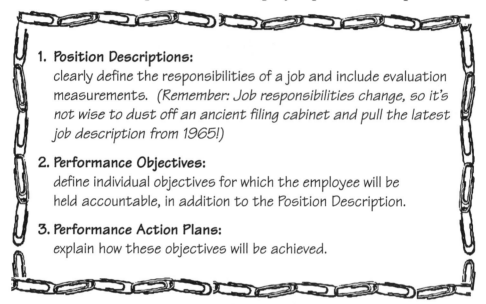

1. **Position Descriptions:**
   clearly define the responsibilities of a job and include evaluation measurements. (Remember: Job responsibilities change, so it's not wise to dust off an ancient filing cabinet and pull the latest job description from 1965!)

2. **Performance Objectives:**
   define individual objectives for which the employee will be held accountable, in addition to the Position Description.

3. **Performance Action Plans:**
   explain how these objectives will be achieved.

In the Coaching Phase, the agreed-upon performance plans are implemented. This is far from being a passive activity. As a team leader, you provide what your team members would have difficulty providing for themselves—a diagnosis of performance needs, on-going direction and support, and frequent feedback to reinforce or redirect efforts.

Of course, throughout the process you're also documenting how your team members are doing. Why would you want to do that? For one, because when you begin the Evaluating Phase and do performance evaluations, they'll be so much *easier.*

The Performance Management Cycle is, in reality, a part of an even larger process—the Measurement Linkage Model, described in *Measuring Organizational Improvement Impact,* also published by Richard Chang Associates, Inc.

The Measurement Linkage Model links organizational goals and objectives to work-group and individual performance by establishing Key Result Areas *(KRAs)* and Key Indicators *(KIs)*. Refer to *Measuring Organizational Improvement Impact* if you want additional information.

MEASUREMENT LINKAGE MODEL

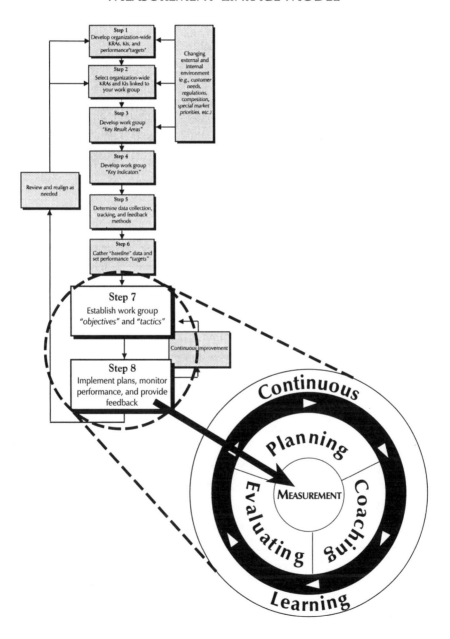

The Real Purpose Of Performance Evaluation

Ask ten managers and you'll probably get ten different reasons for performance evaluations, some legitimate and some less legitimate, that are beyond the scope of this guidebook. At a minimum, performance evaluations provide an opportunity for you and your team members to talk about how things are going on the job. However, the underlying purpose is much deeper.

Performance evaluation provides a way to describe how your team members have performed on the job, and how they can improve their performance in the future so that they, you, and your organization all benefit. It also provides an opportunity to mutually develop work objectives and ways to achieve them. And, of course, it provides documentation to support all personnel decisions *(e.g., promotions, salary adjustments, terminations, etc.)*. These written records may prove useful in resolving possible issues that arise in the future.

Your evaluations of your team members' on-the-job performance should be viewed much like photographs taken of people vacationing together. The photographs *(like your "pictures" of job performance)* represent a place where both parties have already been. There should be no surprises *(after all, both parties were there)*. And the vacationers only took selected photographs to capture key memories; therefore, they don't have a picture for every single moment—just highlights.

As vacationers discuss their photographs at length when they first develop them, you also must discuss job performance with your employees as situations develop. You talk about what went well and what didn't, and what should be done differently. Until then, the photographs sit in storage, like historic documents of places traveled.

Likewise, your completed performance evaluations sit in employee document files. They're looked at when there's a need. Like photographs from a past vacation, it would be borderline *"boring"* to look at or discuss past performance evaluations too often, since both parties have seen them before, and they've both been there. *"Boring" (defined as "been there, done that"),* however, can be good regarding performance evaluations, since it implies that you're having conversations about subject matter you've discussed many times before—you're rehashing old ground.

In Chapter Six, you'll learn how to make these discussions interesting, interactive, and rewarding. But for now, strive for *"boring"*—meaning *absolutely no surprises*—and build from there!

Managers often close their office doors for weeks working on performance evaluations for their team members. Why not involve those whom you're describing?

Do a mental somersault, and change your perspective from a leader-centered performance evaluation to one that is team-member centered. After all, it's *their* evaluation, not yours. Get your employees involved as soon as possible. Share the process and its rewards. *(Chapters Three to Six offer numerous suggestions on how to get team members involved in the performance-evaluation process.)*

Types Of Performance Evaluation

There are numerous times team leaders and members may participate in documenting past individual and team performance. Some types of performance evaluation follow. The tools and techniques covered throughout this guidebook are directly applicable to *all* of them.

Introductory Performance Evaluations

Introductory performance evaluations are often conducted between one to six months after an employee's hire date to determine if the employee is a match for the job. *(Some organizations call it a "probationary" review—a term to be avoided because of its negative connotations. If necessary, use this term to refer to "Corrective Actions." See Chapter Seven.)*

Annual Performance Evaluations

Annual performance evaluations are what everyone usually gets so worked up about. This formal annual documentation of performance highlights *(or "low lights")* strongly influences personnel decisions and ends up in a special employee file *(forever and ever)*.

Special Performance Evaluations

Special performance evaluations are similar to the annual evaluations, except that they're conducted on an *"as-needed"* basis at the request of the team leader or member. Usually, these evaluations support employment status changes such as a role redefinition, change in supervisor or direction, salary adjustment, promotion, etc.

Corrective Actions

Often called *"reprimands,"* these evaluations are a form of progressive discipline, and will be covered in Chapter Seven.

Feedback Sessions

Feedback sessions are informal evaluations of on-the-job performance that take place during the day-to-day coaching process between team leaders and members. Notes taken during these sessions are often placed in employee files that are maintained by the team leader. You'll use these notes when you prepare for your annual performance appraisals, status reports, etc.

Status Reports

Status reports are periodic *(e.g., weekly, monthly, quarterly)* progress reports that are typically submitted to management to document key individual and team performance highlights.

The Tremendous Benefits To Gain

If performance evaluation seems like too much work or involves too many negatives, don't despair. There really are numerous benefits. Consider the following:

◆ Performance will improve by redirecting undesirable behaviors through constructive feedback, and can be maintained and leveraged by reinforcing desirable behaviors through recognition and rewards. Clearer direction, increased motivation, and higher quality results are achieved.

◆ Performance evaluation provides an opportunity to build strong working relationships between you and your team members. If you do the prep work, you'll learn more about your team members' personal goals, ambitions, and attitudes toward their jobs, their careers, and the organization.

◆ Team members' roles and responsibilities can be clarified, especially those areas you consider strengths or those that need improvement. Future performance expectations can be agreed to up-front.

◆ Plans can be created to develop team members' performance in current assignments and prepare them for additional responsibilities *(see Chapter Five)*.

◆ Finally, performance evaluations become historical documents that can later support personnel decisions *(e.g., promotions, demotions, transfers, compensation adjustments, terminations, etc.)*.

Forms (And Formalities)

Performance-evaluation forms vary significantly with levels and types of jobs, organizations, and industries. And not one is loved by all. *"Victims"* whine about a review form that they feel is poorly designed. Chances are, they're partially right, but don't join their crusade. It often takes an act of Congress to change such documents, and you know how long that takes. Besides, there's no perfect form unless, of course, *you* design it!

The bottom line: use any form that best facilitates a discussion between you and your team member regarding past performance and future development plans.

If you don't have a choice, use your organization's form. Don't fight it. You can make *any* form work for you if you follow the guidelines outlined within Chapters Three to Six. Or, you could even use a blank piece of paper, as long as you address these five essential components:

Five essential components

 Performance Plans
This section includes a Position Description, Performance Objectives, and Performance Action Plans—all developed before and during the evaluation period. If you have this information, simply attach it and pat yourself on the back for your up-front planning. *(Refer to **Planning Successful Employee Performance**.)*

 Descriptions Of Performance
This section includes information drawn from many sources including your employee document files *(information you've collected on your team members' performance)*. This is definitely essential information for those who don't have a photographic memory. *(Refer to Coaching For Peak Employee Performance, and see Chapters Three and Four of this guidebook.)*

 Areas Of Strength
Describe areas in which your team members have excelled during the last performance period. Remember, behaviors you recognize and reward will be maintained and leveraged! Make sure that this section has at least as much content as the one that follows. *(See Chapter Four.)*

 Areas Of Needed Improvement
Awareness and understanding precede improvement. People can't improve what they don't know about. In this section, describe in specific terms what they need to stop doing, start doing, or improve. *(See Chapter Four.)*

Employee Development Profiles
This section is important because it looks forward. It's future-focused. Ask yourself, *"What will prepare my team members for additional responsibility?"* It might include such things as challenging assignments or on-the-job training. *(See Chapter Five.)*

The following components of performance evaluations are optional, yet can be valuable inclusions in a performance-evaluation form.

Optional components

 Traits
Many traits are difficult to describe in behavioral terms. *"Courage"* or *"creativity"* can mean many different things to different people. However, assessing traits can be valuable if your organization wants to encourage them as a part of your organization's *"culture."* *(See Chapter Four for how to describe traits in behavioral terms.)*

 Organization Goals And Values
If the success and health of an organization depends on employee contributions to key goals and core values, why not promote them during the annual performance evaluation? One good example is *"customer satisfaction."* An organization may evaluate its people on how well they satisfy their internal and external customers to encourage behaviors that lead to greater customer loyalty. It's also a way to ensure that people are *"doing the right things,"* not just *"doing things right."* *(See Chapter Four for how to reinforce goals and values while describing on-the-job behaviors.)*

Career Interests And Plans
Your team members have goals, interests, and talents, even if they're unspoken. Showing an interest in your team members' career goals is a way to foster trust, and may give you additional insights on how to motivate them. It's recommended that this discussion be conducted soon after the performance evaluation to give it the separate and private attention it deserves. *(See Chapter Six.)*

Employee Comments
This is where team members can add whatever they like, so comments can run the gamut from, *"I'm sure glad I'm a part of this team,"* to *"I do not agree with portions of this performance evaluation."* Yes, it can also include rebuttals and grievances. *(See Chapter Six.)*

Your organization's performance-evaluation form may have other sections for documenting future performance plans, employment status changes *(e.g., salary adjustments, transfers, and promotions)*, etc. This guidebook will focus on the five essential components to help you gain the greatest benefits *(while avoiding the deepest pitfalls).*

The Performance Evaluation Model

If you're interested in a process that takes you all the way to an effective performance evaluation, then look at the following four steps of the Performance Evaluation Model. A word of warning, though: following these steps takes a heavy dose of self-discipline. But the good news is that it will be well worth it. Remember, you can't get a good return on an investment unless you invest!

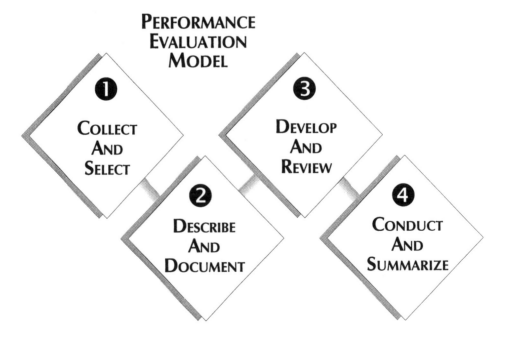

PERFORMANCE EVALUATION MODEL

1 COLLECT AND SELECT

2 DESCRIBE AND DOCUMENT

3 DEVELOP AND REVIEW

4 CONDUCT AND SUMMARIZE

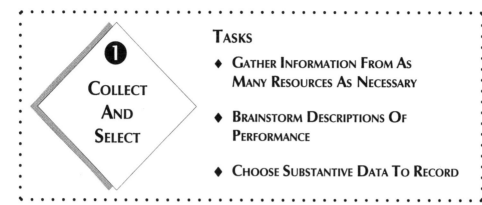

1

COLLECT AND SELECT

TASKS

♦ **GATHER INFORMATION FROM AS MANY RESOURCES AS NECESSARY**

♦ **BRAINSTORM DESCRIPTIONS OF PERFORMANCE**

♦ **CHOOSE SUBSTANTIVE DATA TO RECORD**

During this step, you'll quickly find out how well you've managed your team members' performance during the last evaluation period. The assumption is that you'll have something to collect and select, like notes you've maintained regarding your team members' performance. Next, you'll need to critically evaluate and interpret the meaning of the data, and decide what stands out as being the most significant to include within your documentation. *(See Chapter Three.)*

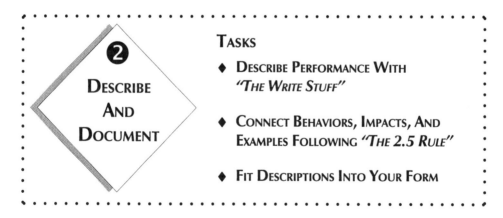

2

DESCRIBE AND DOCUMENT

TASKS

♦ **DESCRIBE PERFORMANCE WITH *"THE WRITE STUFF"***

♦ **CONNECT BEHAVIORS, IMPACTS, AND EXAMPLES FOLLOWING *"THE 2.5 RULE"***

♦ **FIT DESCRIPTIONS INTO YOUR FORM**

In this step, you'll clarify the words that best describe your team members' performance behaviors. Your final descriptions will then be incorporated into the appropriate sections of your organization's form. *(See Chapter Four.)*

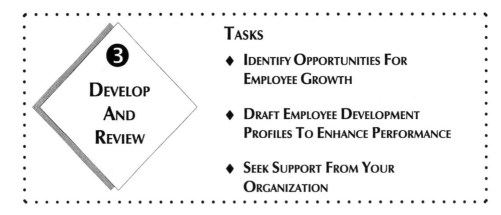

You and your team members will look forward in this step—identifying opportunities for them to expand skills. Collectively, you'll draft initial profiles outlining how they can capitalize on their areas of strength, and how they can improve. Finally, you'll have others within your organization approve your documentation before the performance-evaluation meeting. *(See Chapter Five.)*

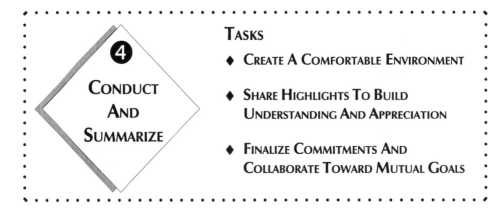

What used to be the hard part now becomes easy, because you've invested the time up-front. You'll choose a meeting place that can provide comfort and privacy, and you'll share highlights of your team members' past performance, as well as finalize future performance commitments. The only thing that's left is to begin collaborating toward mutually agreed-upon goals. *(See Chapter Six.)*

These four steps in the Performance Evaluation Model will lead you toward developing effective performance evaluations. Along the way, you and your team members will gain self confidence in the area of employee evaluation, and the improved performance of your team members will encourage you and them to stick with the steps. It takes a combination of work, practice, and insight, but the results will keep you going.

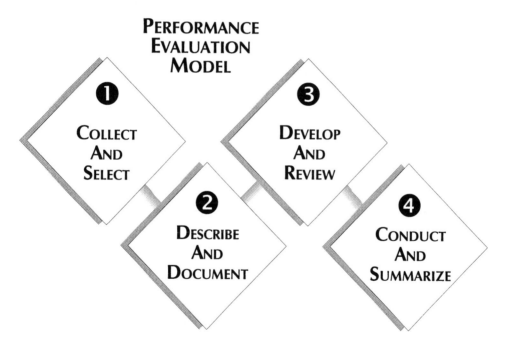

PERFORMANCE
EVALUATION
MODEL

❶ COLLECT AND SELECT

❷ DESCRIBE AND DOCUMENT

❸ DEVELOP AND REVIEW

❹ CONDUCT AND SUMMARIZE

CHAPTER TWO WORKSHEET: ASSESSING YOUR ORGANIZATION'S PERFORMANCE-EVALUATION PROCESS

1. Describe your organization's performance-evaluation process.

_____

_____

_____

_____

_____

_____

_____

2. How do you currently plan for performance evaluations?

_____

_____

_____

_____

_____

_____

_____

3. Look at the steps and tasks listed within the Performance Evaluation Model. Check which steps and tasks are currently part of your performance-evaluation process.

☐ ❶ **COLLECT AND SELECT**

   ☐ **GATHER INFORMATION FROM AS MANY RESOURCES AS NECESSARY**

   ☐ **BRAINSTORM DESCRIPTIONS OF PERFORMANCE**

   ☐ **CHOOSE SUBSTANTIVE DATA TO RECORD**

☐ ❷ **DESCRIBE AND DOCUMENT**

   ☐ **DESCRIBE PERFORMANCE WITH "THE WRITE STUFF"**

   ☐ **CONNECT BEHAVIORS, IMPACTS, AND EXAMPLES FOLLOWING "THE 2.5 RULE"**

   ☐ **FIT DESCRIPTIONS INTO YOUR FORM**

☐ ❸ **DEVELOP AND REVIEW**

   ☐ **IDENTIFY OPPORTUNITIES FOR EMPLOYEE GROWTH**

   ☐ **DRAFT EMPLOYEE DEVELOPMENT PROFILES TO ENHANCE PERFORMANCE**

   ☐ **SEEK SUPPORT FROM YOUR ORGANIZATION**

☐ ❹ **CONDUCT AND SUMMARIZE**

   ☐ **CREATE A COMFORTABLE ENVIRONMENT**

   ☐ **SHARE HIGHLIGHTS TO BUILD UNDERSTANDING AND APPRECIATION**

   ☐ **FINALIZE COMMITMENTS AND COLLABORATE TOWARD MUTUAL GOALS**

COLLECT AND SELECT

①

COLLECT AND SELECT

TASKS

♦ **GATHER INFORMATION FROM AS MANY RESOURCES AS NECESSARY**

♦ **BRAINSTORM DESCRIPTIONS OF PERFORMANCE**

♦ **CHOOSE SUBSTANTIVE DATA TO RECORD**

Tools

Performance Evaluation Preparation Checklist

Performance Evaluation Thought Jogger

How do you begin? Don't write. Don't start with the form staring at you. Don't let your eyes water, your mind wander, and your time squander.

Professional journalists rarely start by typing the first paragraph of their column. Professional novelists rarely start by developing the first paragraph of Chapter One. Why?

It's much more difficult, if not impossible for some, to put together a puzzle without having an idea of what the final picture should look like or without the confidence that they have all the pieces.

Writers of employee evaluations often make this same mistake. They start with their organization's performance evaluation in front of them. They gaze at the paper form or computer-screen display with a blank stare, hoping that something will happen. But it doesn't. They can't think of what to write.

Professional writers would rather have a lot of ideas from which to condense, than the other way around. A writer of romantic novels may not know the beginning, direction, or ending of his story, but he'll often begin by collecting *"golden nuggets"* *(essential information)* that he will fit somewhere within the story line later—e.g., *"the characters have to be quirky and edgy, but believable; the locations have to be dark and mysterious, yet familiar; and there has to be romance for it to sell!"*

Usually, the only person who thinks the way an evaluation form is designed is the person who created it. So get the form out of sight, and begin gathering critical data about your employee's performance over the past review period.

Don't have time to gather data? Some people are convinced that sinister forces are at work to make their lives miserable. They often make comments like this:

> They always *do* these things at the end of the year when we're the most busy.

> I have ten of these things to do—how do they expect me to get them all done in this short time frame?

Whiners! They sound like victims, don't they? Don't blame the administrator of the process for not giving you enough time. This is *your* responsibility. Create your own reminder systems *(e.g., mark your calendars)* to allow you and others as much time as you collectively need for research, preparation, and approvals.

Gather Information From As Many Resources As Necessary

If you followed the advice in *Planning Successful Employee Performance* and *Coaching For Peak Employee Performance,* the process of developing a performance evaluation will be easier. You'll be gathering information a little bit at a time, over the entire performance period. If you think that's tough, try writing a dozen performance evaluations with no more to go on than your memory, good looks, and a prayer.

What you write in your performance evaluations must be complete, and supported by solid research and objective information. But where do you get the information? Start by gathering it from all of the sources that are available to you. Then you will be fully prepared to write your comments.

Use the following Performance Evaluation Preparation Checklist as a reference back on the job, to help you collect information to incorporate in your next employee performance evaluation.

PERFORMANCE EVALUATION PREPARATION CHECKLIST

**Consider using the sources below as you collect information
for an upcoming employee performance evaluation.**

❏ 1. Employee's self-evaluation.

◆ *Employees can be realistic about their strengths and weaknesses. Weigh the employee's self-assessments against other information.*

❏ 2. Employee performance plan (*i.e., Position Description, Performance Objectives, Performance Action Plans; See **Planning Successful Employee Performance** guidebook.*)

❏ 3. Current list of job assignments/projects.

❏ 4. Observations of current performance.

◆ *Complete the Performance Evaluation Thought Jogger.*

◆ *Collect Performance Progress Sheet(s) that were completed during the performance period (i.e., your ongoing coaching notes. See **Coaching For Peak Employee Performance** guidebook).*

❏ 5. Strategic business plans *(e.g., visions, missions, core values, strategies, goals, objectives, tactics, etc.).*

❏ 6. Project charts/schedules, activity/progress/status reports, and administrative memos and letters.

◆ *These accessible documents may provide consistent detailed records of key employee and team accomplishments, actions, events, and incidents.*

❏ 7. Previous performance evaluations.

◆ *Determine if last year's performance expectations were met, and why or why not. Review other information for useful information and patterns. Don't assume accuracy.*

❏ 8. Customer-satisfaction surveys and other forms of feedback.

❏ 9. Human Resources/Personnel files (*e.g., including employment-status changes, letters from internal/external customers, etc.*).

❏ 10. Feedback from others (*e.g., former supervisors, coworkers, contractors, consultants, direct reports, suppliers, and customers*).

◆ *Weigh these views against other information. This information is useful if the employee worked a portion of the review period under another supervisor, closely with employees in other departments, etc.*

❏ 11. Changes that may have affected the employee's performance:

◆ *Organizational*   ◆ *Relationships with customers, suppliers, etc.*
◆ *Staffing*   ◆ *Departmental procedures*
◆ *Budget*   ◆ *Employee performance plans*
◆ *Schedule*   ◆ *Company policy or business law*
◆ *Facility*   ◆ *Critical personal incidents (w/ caution!, e.g.,*
◆ *Market/competition*   *"was on approved LOA")*

Using selected sources of information

As you gather data for performance evaluations, beware of how, when, where, why, and from whom you ask. The following three excerpts from the Performance Evaluation Preparation Checklist will illustrate some of the challenges and the benefits from gathering information.

Employee's self-evaluation *(# 1 from checklist)*

It's a good idea to include an employee self-evaluation because your team members can be valuable contributors to their own performance evaluations. That doesn't sound too radical, does it?

Of course, there are good ways and bad ways of going about it. For example:

> It's review time. We're supposed to ask for your input. Here. Fill this out and get it to me by the end of the week.

Wow! Inspiring, eh? A better approach:

> I'd like to ensure we have all the information we need, including your own views of your performance. Will you please complete a self-evaluation within the next few weeks? I'd like to use it as one of the key data points when I draft your performance evaluation.

Surprisingly, most team members will be hard on themselves. Harder than you would be on them. Yes, a few employees may see this as an advantage to *"inflate their scores"* and write a better review than they deserve. But you'll have to address this *"perception void"* later anyway, so you're better off knowing in advance exactly where the two of you agree and differ. And, frankly, maybe a few of their perspectives will change yours.

Laurie Allison is Director of New Technologies...

for a small entrepreneurial computer firm that develops multimedia software for the Internet. She considers every one of her team members to be very competent and self-directed. They have to be, in a crazy environment where only the paranoid survive. Six months ago, she snatched Benjamin Wells away from a major technology firm, and in two weeks he'll be receiving his first performance evaluation. Laurie likes to involve her team members in the process. She reasons, *"They're professionals, and more times than not, are involved in things I'm not up to speed on."*

Laurie explained to Benjamin what she expected. *"What I'd like for you to do is share your thoughts on your performance over the past year by completing our performance-evaluation form. I'd like to include your ideas within my data collection."*

Benjamin appeared shocked. *"This is your job, not mine,"* he retorted. *"Besides, I'm a programmer, not a personnel clerk."*

"Yes, Benjamin," Laurie interjected, *"it's my job to ensure your performance is documented. But it's your performance review. It's to our advantage that you're a part of it. What if I've forgotten about a key accomplishment or I've overlooked a significant effort? I need your help. I not only want to know about projects you've worked on, but where you think your time can best be spent in the future. I've prepared a supplemental list of questions to help you. Most are asking for your ideas on how I can support you better."*

Benjamin paused, then added, *"Hmm, I can probably think of a few things."*

Laurie smiled. *"I have no doubt you will,"* she replied. *"If you need help in the next couple of weeks, please see me."*

Veteran workers may miss the benefits of their participation. New hires may find self-appraisals threatening. In either case, sell them on how a self-evaluation will be used to everyone's benefit. Give employees as much notice as necessary—they'll likely have a full plate and don't want to be stressed with this additional task in a tight time frame.

You also may need to allocate time to train your team members on how to use your organization's form. *(Note: Give employees the same form you have to fill out. This will train them to be future team leaders as they develop the necessary skills and understanding required to successfully complete your organization's form. This will also make your job of synthesizing data much easier!)* Provide your team members with all the help you can—notes, suggestions, references, examples, questions to stimulate thoughts, even this practical guidebook—to make their job *(and yours)* easier.

Feedback from others *(#10 from checklist)*

Don't be shy about asking other people for performance data. Sometimes it's absolutely necessary *(e.g., when a new supervisor needs information from the previous supervisor who managed an employee's performance for a significant portion of the review period).* Or maybe it's just a case of a *"highly-evolved manager"* who wants to get a few more facts on her team members' performance.

Consider offering others various ways of helping you retrieve this information. The easier you make it on them, the more likely you'll receive what you want. Some options:

- ◆ Have them write notes directly on your organization's performance-evaluation form.

- ◆ Interview others while you take notes *(e.g., directly on the Performance Evaluation Thought Jogger, explained on the following pages).*

- ◆ Develop and use a special assessment tool *(like a survey)* created for the job you're reviewing to collect data that is easier to synthesize.

Fulvio Sanchez is a new supervisor...

at a large manufacturing company that produces aerospace parts. He found himself in the difficult position of having to write a performance evaluation for Julianna Hines, one of his team members. Unfortunately, he only had two months of data on Julianna's performance. He decided to try and reach Julianna's former supervisor, Kelly Conley, who had moved to another organization. Fulvio thought about sending Kelly the evaluation form to complete, but decided against it because if it were him, he probably wouldn't fill it out. Out of sight, out of mind.

After a week of trying, he finally tracked her down by phone.

"Kelly, I'd like to ask you a few questions about Julianna's performance during the last ten months you were her supervisor," Fulvio began.

Kelly stalled. *"My memory's not what it used to be,"* she replied.

"Not to worry," Fulvio assured her. *" I've got a list of questions that might spark some ideas for you. First, what was one of her greatest strengths?*

Kelly thought for a moment and then said, *"As I recall, Julianna always produced quality work. Though she had some difficulty meeting output standards . . ."*

"Why?" Fulvio probed, following with more targeted questions. He noted Kelly's thoughts as she opened up with a good twenty minutes of essential feedback.

By conversation's end, Fulvio had enough information to complete Julianna's performance evaluation. He noted that Julianna's earlier problem with meeting standards was completely resolved. Fulvio also suggested to Human Resources that future *"losses"* of historic performance data could be avoided if supervisors who were leaving the organization *(or leadership position)* had to complete performance evaluations for their team members *before* they left.

Much like the journalist or novelist, you don't have to use everything that you gather. But you'll feel more comfortable having a lot to sift through than having an empty sifter.

You may receive performance data that seems to contradict your own observations. Often, it's a matter of varying definitions, requirements, or expectations. Try to resolve these differences by looking and listening for trends.

Since an employee's performance can change over time, note performance feedback within the review by time period and evaluator. You are capturing historical data—and this is a key part of history.

For example, note who else supervised your team member, and when. Also include these former supervisors' descriptions of your employee's performance during those times, directly on the performance evaluation form. Then, follow with your descriptions of the employee's performance under your supervision.

Finally, tell your team member *and* all others from whom you are gathering data that you will *not* use all information you collect *(you will only synthesize trends and significant events)*. You also will maintain complete confidentiality *(you will not tell the evaluated employee who said what)*. Otherwise, your team member's coworkers and direct reports will be understandably apprehensive about sharing information.

Changes that may have affected the employee's performance *(# 11 from checklist)*

Note any significant changes that may have affected your employee's performance, even if you and the team member are positive and comfortable as to what happened and why. Memories will fade, but your documentation will last for years.

For instance, if your team member didn't complete an assignment because of an organizational restructuring *(budget cut, job transfer, etc.)* that changed the individual's or team's priorities, the performance evaluation should say exactly that. If the employee was not on the job for a period of time, simply document the absence *(e.g., "Laurie was on an approved leave of absence from xx/xx/xx to xx/xx/xx."),* without getting into all the personal reasons why. *(These reasons may be important to document within the leave-of-absence request form, but do not belong on a performance evaluation.)*

In the Appendix, you'll find a reproducible version of the Performance Evaluation Preparation Checklist. Use it as you begin your data collection.

Brainstorm Descriptions Of Performance

When people update their resumes, they often follow someone else's format. The final product may look good, and it may even pass all guidelines considered desirable and acceptable. Even so, the resume may not clearly highlight the key reasons why the person should be hired. So he's not.

The same holds true with performance evaluations. People often follow someone else's format, complete entire evaluations, and then, when confronted by employees with the fact that it doesn't seem to represent what was said about them all year long, these managers respond with, *"The form didn't ask for that."* Should you blame the form?

No. Avoid that mental trap. Think. You likely have five, ten, even twenty or more ideas off the top of your head that you know should be *somewhere* within a team member's performance evaluation. Don't worry about where an idea will eventually fit. And don't concern yourself with word choice at this time. Don't even wonder whether or not an idea is good enough to use. Just write them all down, *starting now, while they're fresh!* Don't be surprised if you have thirty to fifty rough ideas captured in about thirty minutes!

The following Performance Evaluation Thought Jogger can help trigger some ideas. Write single words or phrases—you'll clarify these *"descriptions"* later. In the Appendix, you'll find a blank Performance Evaluation Thought Jogger and some word lists—*"Describing Skills And Traits"*—that will help you generate more ideas.

The Performance Evaluation Thought Jogger on the following page has been partially completed to give you an idea of how to use it.

PERFORMANCE EVALUATION THOUGHT JOGGER

THIS TEAM MEMBER SHOULD:

DO MORE
- taking initiative for solving problems
- scoping project milestones
- delegating work activities
- negotiating for better pricing

CONTINUE TO
- be a team player
- be innovative
- be quality-driven
- pursue outside educational opportunities

DO LESS
- "ABC" activities
- asking for permission
- using support services
- "freelance" work for other departments without proper documentation first

LEARN ABOUT
- new computer software applications (especially spreadsheets)
- internal customer problems
- department budgeting process
- product mix

START
- meeting regularly with internal customers
- leading work-group meetings
- making customer visits
- measuring objectives

ASSUME RESPONSIBILITY FOR
- leading projects
- team-member development activities
- coordinating with suppliers
- overseeing cost/benefit analyses

STOP
- missing project deadlines
- trying to do too much
- cost overruns
- accepting new work assignments

OTHER
- look for opportunities to develop new "XYZ" skills
- complete monthly activity report
- present topic at department's annual "kickoff" meeting
- attend two public seminars

GENERAL DESCRIPTIONS ABOUT THIS TEAM MEMBER'S PERFORMANCE:

PLUSES
- very creative and innovative
- quality work
- helpful and considerate team member
- enjoys learning new skills

MINUSES
- misses deadlines
- tries to do too much
- reluctant to lead projects
- manages time inefficiently

Choose Substantive Data To Record

At this point, you should have a stack of data in front of you, including your own brainstorming notes. Don't be overwhelmed. Simply select what data to include, what to combine, what to defer, and what to trash.

What follows are some decision criteria to help you choose what data to include:

1. Seek data that supports trends. For example, *"This team member completes projects under budget."*

2. Consider including *"significant events"* in a team member's performance if the impacts of her performance are significant. Maybe, in one act of brilliance, she saved the organization a cool million. Or, heaven forbid, during one mental lapse, he cost the team its key customer.

3. Lean toward factual and first-hand information. Avoid rumors, assumptions, and distortions.

Follow the *"80/20 Rule"* to reduce your Performance Evaluation Thought Jogger list from thirty to fifty rough ideas down to six to ten or more. The *"80/20 Rule"* says that of all the data you collect, 20 percent includes *"golden nuggets"* that account for 80 percent of your team member's results. These more significant performance observations should be included in your performance evaluation documentation.

Golden Nuggets

Non-nuggets

With this preparation, you'll be off to a great start. *(At the very least, you'll have enough "golden nuggets" to fill a gold mine.)* Keep going. In the next chapter, you'll go right *(write)* to the evaluation form.

CHAPTER THREE WORKSHEET: STARTING YOUR COLLECTION

1. Make a copy of the Performance Evaluation Preparation Checklist in the Appendix, and begin collecting information on a team member's performance.

   a. Check the sources on the Performance Evaluation Preparation Checklist you think will be most useful.

   b. List who can provide additional data on your team member's performance, and how you will gather this information from each of these sources.

   _____

   _____

   _____

   _____

   c. Identify the questions you will ask to help others help you fill in the performance history *"gaps."*

   _____

   _____

   _____

   _____

2. Use the Performance Evaluation Thought Jogger to brainstorm your thoughts and ideas about a team member's performance.

PERFORMANCE EVALUATION THOUGHT JOGGER	
THIS TEAM MEMBER SHOULD:	
DO MORE	**CONTINUE TO**
DO LESS	**LEARN ABOUT**
START	**ASSUME RESPONSIBILITY FOR**
STOP	**OTHER**
GENERAL DESCRIPTIONS ABOUT THIS TEAM MEMBER'S PERFORMANCE:	
PLUSES	**MINUSES**

3. Begin to select your team member's most significant performance areas during the evaluation period. Use the *"80/20 Rule"* to circle the *"golden nuggets"* on the Performance Evaluation Thought Jogger in Question # 2. *(Continue this selection process once you've collected more performance data from others.)*

DESCRIBE AND DOCUMENT

②

DESCRIBE AND DOCUMENT

TASKS

♦ **DESCRIBE PERFORMANCE WITH "THE WRITE STUFF"**

♦ **CONNECT BEHAVIORS, IMPACTS, AND EXAMPLES FOLLOWING "THE 2.5 RULE"**

♦ **FIT DESCRIPTIONS INTO YOUR FORM**

You don't have to write prose like William Shakespeare, or even your high school English teacher, to complete a performance evaluation. It's more important that you can describe your team members' on-the-job performance and impacts clearly and accurately. Save your creative juices for that screenplay you want to write someday.

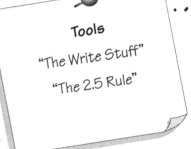

Tools

"The Write Stuff"

"The 2.5 Rule"

Describe Performance With "The Write Stuff"

The problem with many comments found on performance evaluations is that they say very little, and can be interpreted in a number of ways. Here's a *"tongue-in-cheek"* look at comments taken directly from real evaluation forms, and what they *could* mean:

> ☞ *"Bill continues to support Project 'XYZ.'"*
>
> **Meaning:** Bill's still working on the stupid thing. No one really knows exactly what he does. He won't lift a finger to help elsewhere. *(Consider expanding with, "Bill continues to breathe.")*

☞ *"Andrea is invaluable to our organization and should be considered for promotion."*

Meaning: We want her out of here—she's driving us crazy! You can consider her all day long for a promotion—*"she just ain't getting one."* We can't afford to give her a raise, so we'll see if this comment will pacify her for now.

☞ *"Doug should be more of a team player. He should take a class on 'Team Building.'"*

Meaning: He's not getting *my* work done. He doesn't let me get in the final word. We want him to do more things we can't measure. We want to boost class enrollments.

☞ *"Carter gets along well with others because he's a good communicator."*

Meaning: We don't know what the heck he's talking about, but we like him anyway. He talks his way out of work. He uses big words that impress my boss.

These comments may remind you of when a politician speaks. Sounds okay. Makes you feel good. Doesn't say zilch. May haunt you later.

The only good news about the *"sounds good—says nothing"* comments is that they *do* take up space on the form, giving the writer the *impression* that she's getting the darn thing done. Don't fool yourself. Provide more precise descriptions of your team members' behaviors.

Victor Chung manages...

a major department store. Gabrielle DeGeronimo runs the home-furnishing department. Their relationship could be described as tense. It's not that Gabrielle isn't capable; she is. In fact, her department is consistently rated as the best managed. Their personalities just seem to clash.

Victor is in the middle of a performance evaluation with Gabrielle. He's always tried to balance *"Areas Of Strength"* with *"Areas Of Needed Improvement."* And it has always worked—until now.

Victor, trying to develop Gabrielle during her performance evaluation, recommends, " *As far as improvement opportunities, I'd like you to be more assertive when you..."*

Gabrielle doesn't let Victor finish his sentence. *"What do you mean I'm not assertive?"* she interrupts, *"I constantly confront you privately on issues on which we don't agree. I handle all customer complaints directly. I deal with poor performance on my staff immediately, firmly, and professionally."*

Victor diplomatically responds with, *"Gabrielle, please. You're getting upset and defensive. I don't know why you're having such a problem with one low rating. Your overall performance is above average and..."*

"Upset?" Gabrielle erupts. *"Yes, with your 'above average' overall rating of my work—a gross understatement. And that 'one low rating' is a career 'kiss of death' around here. But, am I defensive? No. I'm just protecting myself from the sharp hook while you fish. You think that in order to balance the scales, you have to fish for something wrong with my performance, even if it's not there. Makes you look like a 'tough' manager."*

Victor: *"Now wait just one minute..."*

Gabrielle: *"Give me one example of when you think I was not being assertive."*

Victor: *"You're not being assertive right now! You're being aggressive!"*

Gabrielle: *"Oh, great! We've now moved on to another 'label' for my directness."*

Victor, Victor, Victor. It doesn't have to be like this. Instead, *"Write right!"* Direct, accurate, and sincere feedback is appreciated by all team members, and you owe it to them. Just use *"The Write Stuff"*— valuable tips to help you write meaningful comments on your team members' performance evaluations.

"The Write Stuff"

1. Use simple journalism.

Describe observable behavior with short, familiar, precise, and accurate words. It should be more challenging to make the message simple and understandable, rather than complex and difficult.

For example:

♦ Completed "XYZ" experiments three weeks ahead of schedule

♦ Went over budget by 15 percent on Project "ABC"

♦ Completed certification three days before scheduled deadline

2. Strive for accuracy.

Be honest and objective, yet avoid going out of your way to hurt people's feelings in the process of providing detailed constructive feedback.

For example:

Instead of, *"Scott is losing the 'ABC' Account because he is unresponsive to our customers,"* be a little more diplomatic and a little less judgmental. Try:

Scott was perceived by 'ABC' customer as not quickly responding to their requests. As a result, 'ABC' customer said they are considering taking their business to a competitor.

3. **Ensure consistency.**

Your oral and written descriptions should support one another. Avoid sending mixed, conflicting, or surprising messages. *(Check your notes in your employee files, and read through the documentation from your coaching feedback sessions.)*

4. **Maintain confidentiality.**

Don't disclose anything that will expose you and your organization to legal risks *(e.g., saying: "You got a lower rating than Shannon," or writing: "Jan should be promoted").* When in doubt, check with Human Resources, senior management, etc., for a second opinion.

5. **Be direct, yet non-confrontational.**

To accomplish this goal:

a. Focus on describing your employees' specific behaviors, rather than judging their personalities.

For example:

> When you don't speak up in our meetings, it looks to our team like you are not interested in the topic.
>
> (instead of: "You're not interested. It's because of your bad attitude.")

b. Use the word *"perception"* when discussing another person's views of your team members' performance.

For example:

> Some managers perceive that you are unresponsive when you don't return phone calls within two hours.
>
> (instead of: "You are unresponsive.")

c. Use facts, examples, direct quotes, and data to support your conclusions or criticisms.

For example:

> You were twenty minutes late three times in the past thirty calendar days.
>
> (instead of: "You are always late.")

Many more guidelines for sharing constructive feedback can be found in the practical guidebook, *Coaching Through Effective Feedback*, published by Richard Chang Associates, Inc.

6. Avoid confusing words.

Technical, inflated, slang, or vague words convey a multitude of meanings. Examples follow.

"Confusing" Words With More Precise Definitions
(To Incorporate Into "2.5 Rule" Descriptions)

MATURE
- remains calm and poised while managing stressful situations
- relies on professional team experience when resolving unfamiliar and complex issues
- considers long-range goals while responding to short-term crises
- constantly sharpens and capitalizes on skill strengths

PATIENT
- handles frustrating situations rationally and calmly
- maintains a balanced perspective while hearing all sides of a story
- can postpone rewards/gratification
- completes detailed, repetitive tasks without complaint

RESPONSIBLE
- has a track record of meeting obligations
- admits mistakes
- is accountable for actions
- takes charge without supervision

AGGRESSIVE
- takes a leadership role
- demonstrates initiative by comfortably stepping into high-risk situations
- can intimidate others with quick and unexplained actions
- prefers control over collaboration

IMPULSIVE
- makes critical decisions quickly before all the facts are in
- does not always stick to a plan of action
- easily sidetracked
- proposes solutions without considering impacts, consequences, or contingencies

INITIATIVE
- constantly finds new and better ways of performing job
- does things without being told and with minimal supervision
- is extremely active and eager to try new approaches
- views problems as opportunities on which to capitalize

LOYAL
- shows intense interest and pride in job
- displays a renewed sense of purpose
- places organizational interests ahead of personal convenience
- builds employee enthusiasm and encourages team-member involvement

Connect Behaviors, Impacts, And Examples Following "The 2.5 Rule"

Instead of writing, *"Karl is organized,"* you need to explain what you mean by *"organized,"* the desirable impacts of his *"organizational"* behaviors, and examples of him applying these *"organizational"* skills on-the-job. In other words, you should follow *"The 2.5 Rule."*

"The 2.5 Rule"

When describing team members' performance in writing, ensure that you use *at least* two and one-half sentences to describe any *"Area Of Strength"* or *"Area Of Needed Improvement."* This *"minimum description"* of a behavior *(skill)* should also supplement any numerical ratings given and boxes checked within your organization's form. The goal is to focus feedback on actual *behaviors* and their impacts on-the-job.

APPLYING "THE 2.5 RULE"

Use a minimum of two and one-half sentences to describe any behavior (skill).

1. BEHAVIOR

Clearly describe the behavior in succinct terms. *(Use at least one full sentence.)*

2. IMPACTS

Specifically explain the impacts of the behavior. *(Use at least one full sentence.)*

Consider including three or more desirable, undesirable, short and/or long-term impacts and consequences of this employee's behavior. Consider impacts to the employee, you, team, organization, customer, etc. This sentence will explain why this behavior is valued as an area of strength, or, why this behavior requires improvement.

(.5) EXAMPLE(S)

Cite at least one to two specific and convincing examples of a project or situation where you observed this behavior as an *"Area Of Strength"* or an *"Area Of Needed Improvement."* *(Use one half sentence—i.e., a phrase in parentheses.)*

EXAMPLES OF BEHAVIORS DESCRIBED FOLLOWING "THE 2.5 RULE"

1. **BEHAVIOR (STRENGTH)**

Alec meets with team members before starting a project to communicate roles, schedules, and priorities to ensure his team is organized and ready to meet the challenges of the project.

2. **IMPACTS**

As a result, budgets and schedules are adhered to, team members and customers are satisfied, and senior managers are freed up to handle other tasks. *(They rely on Alec and trust him.)*

(.5) **EXAMPLE(S)**

(e.g., new project kick-off for the "ABC" and "XYZ" projects.)

---

1. **BEHAVIOR (STRENGTH)**

Scott either meets the date for project completion or negotiates agreeable schedule changes with our customers in advance.

2. **IMPACTS**

As a result, his team and customers can plan adequately to avoid further delays, resulting in more efficient operations and a better working relationship.

(.5) **EXAMPLE(S)**

(e.g., informing the "TBD" Department two weeks in advance of the projected due date that the final project would be three days later than expected due to unanticipated systems problems.)

---

1. **BEHAVIOR (AREA OF NEEDED IMPROVEMENT)**

Chris reviews project progress with internal customers annually or upon their request.

2. **IMPACTS**

As a result, customers share little information with him or his team. Changes to customer requirements are discovered too late for his team to act upon, customer decisions are made that exclude his department, and opportunities to build customer relationships and trust are minimized.

(.5) **EXAMPLE(S)**

(e.g., "XYZ" project with "ABC" internal customer.)

---

1. **BEHAVIOR (AREA OF NEEDED IMPROVEMENT)**

Sean is often the only active speaker and participant in department meetings he leads.

2. **IMPACTS**

As a result, Sean's input—although perceived as value-added—often dominates the discussion, and employees don't feel that their input and opinions are heard or respected. Eventually they cease contributing and merely wait for Sean's direction.

(.5) **EXAMPLE(S)**

(e.g., "ABC" and "XYZ" meetings.)

Take each of your key ideas that you selected in the *"Collect And Select"* step, and expand each one, following *"The 2.5 Rule."* At first, this may seem like a large undertaking, but once you get a hang of writing with this style, you'll find that **it takes less than two minutes to draft "2.5" sentences.** Assuming you will select six to ten or more rough ideas from your Performance Evaluation Thought Jogger, you'll invest twelve-to-twenty minutes in capturing the essence of your data from this source in a first draft! You now have time to add to and revise your ideas.

Don't spend time reinventing the wheel. If you've been documenting your team members' performance all along, use it! Any and all information within your employee document files is fair game, including notes from coaching feedback sessions, Performance Progress Sheets, etc. Go ahead and lift documented behaviors directly from your Performance Progress Sheets, and rewrite them using *"The 2.5 Rule."*

In Chapter Two, it was mentioned that you may be required by your organization to evaluate your team members' performance in relationship to *"traits," "goals,"* or *"values."* No problem. Use the first sentence *(of your description following "The 2.5 Rule")* to clarify the trait, goal, or value as demonstrated in terms of your employees' actual on-the-job behavior *(i.e., what they did).* Use the second sentence to document the impacts of what they did. And follow with an example(s).

Write *(or type on your computer)* your descriptions of behaviors following *"The 2.5 Rule"* in a single list. Don't worry about where everything will fit within your organization's performance evaluation form. Remember the resume analogy on page 30? You should be more concerned that you have all of the critical information you need, than worry about in what section of someone else's form it will fit.

Describing "Areas Of Needed Improvement"

Face it. It's often easier and less threatening to write about *"Areas Of Strength"* versus *"Areas Of Needed Improvement."* However, if you want your team members to improve their performance—practice, practice, practice *"The 2.5 Rule."*

Beware of two traps as you write the first sentence describing a team member's *"Area Of Needed Improvement."* Be cautious of using the words *"not"* and *"needs to."* Their usage can sometimes lead to limited understanding and options for improvement.

CAUTION | Using the word, *"not"*

Using the word, *"not,"* can cause confrontations or be misleading. For example:

> Nick is **not** conducting weekly staff meetings. As a result, his staff is not remaining current with all of the ongoing changes to client requirements, etc.

When Nick hears or reads this, he's likely to do one of two things:

1. His brain will go into *"auto-sort mode,"* looking for one example when he *did* conduct a weekly staff meeting—and blow apart your contention.

—or—

2. He will start scheduling weekly staff meetings. Maybe a good response, but that's not the point. His staff needs to remain current with changes—and there are *many* ways to keep teams up-to-date. But Nick may not be a mind reader.

Sometimes, when you use the word, *"not,"* your team member may not know what he *is* doing and the current undesirable impacts *(i.e., reasons why his behavior needs to be improved)*. And, as a corrective action, he may only do what he's currently *not doing*. Often, that's not enough!

To avoid confusion, consider this alternative:

> Nick is maintaining a private file of client changes to project requirements, and is sharing his notes in monthly staff meetings. As a result, his staff is unfamiliar with ongoing changes to requirements, opportunities to incorporate these changes have been missed, etc.

Now you are describing exactly what Nick *is* doing, and the subsequent impacts. As a *"Development Action"* (a key component of an Employee Development Profile explained in Chapter Five), Nick may find it helpful to meet more often with his staff *(e.g., on a weekly or "as-needed" basis)*. But he and you may also come up with other ways to keep his staff informed *(e.g., maintaining client requirement changes on a fileserver, using voice-mail and e-mail for updating the staff, etc.)*.

There are exceptions. In some cases, it's actually best to use the word *"not."* For example, *"Charisse is not signing the contracts she sends to customers"* sends a clearer message than *"Charisse is sending her customers her contracts with the signature line blank."*

Using the words, "needs to"

Using the words, *"needs to,"* can be presumptuous or lead to resistance. For example:

> Duane **needs to** take a class to learn 'XYZ' spreadsheet software. As a result, he will save time by being more efficient, reduce misunderstandings with coworkers with whom he often shares his budgeting tasks, increase his accuracy, etc.

Duane may be open to this good advice. But you're not describing Duane's *"Area Of Needed Improvement."* You're only telling him one way to improve something currently undefined!

At best, Duane readily learns how to use the software. But this may not resolve all of your concerns with his current performance. At worst, he resents your forcing him to go to a class and to use "XYZ" software *"for no good reason,"* and the undesirable impacts of his current behavior may become progressively worse.

Check out this alternative:

> Duane is maintaining our department budgets using handwritten charts, and tables within word-processing software. As a result, Duane's manual calculations are taking thirty-to-forty hours (versus three-to-four hours) to revise quarterly budgets, coworkers cannot readily take over his files in his absence since they don't know his formulas, and calculation errors have been found in the last four updates.

Yes, this is more direct and may be more uncomfortable for you to share at first. Yet, it's accurate, honest, and non-judgmental. Besides, if Duane were to ask *why* he should take a class and *why* he has to learn "XYZ" spreadsheet software, you'd be in a position to provide this rationale off the top of your head. So why not *"write it right"* the first time?

Save your advice regarding *"going to a class"* and *"choosing 'XYZ' spreadsheet software"* for your discussion with Duane on *how* to address his *"Area Of Needed Improvement" (in the next step–Chapter Five).* You may discover additional *"Development Actions"* as well.

Enforce *"The 2.5 Rule"* and *"The Write Stuff"* within your team to ensure clear communications, succinct performance documentation, and legally sound management practices.

Fit Descriptions Into Your Form

At this point, you've selected ideas that you consider the *"cream of the crop,"* and have expanded upon many of them using *"The 2.5 Rule."* Now, look at your organization's performance-evaluation form.

Every form will have sections. Often these sections will be numbered. If they're not, use a pen and number them now. Use these numbers as codes.

Then put a code on each key research document and/or next to each *"2.5 Rule"* description you've developed. The code represents where, within the form, you feel this information best fits. Everyone will do this a little differently, but it doesn't matter much. What matters *(much like the resume analogy on page 30)* is that somewhere within your completed performance evaluation will be *"The Write Stuff."* No longer will the form run the show; *you* will run the show.

For example, what if in the *"Do More"* section of your Performance Evaluation Thought Jogger, you wrote, *"taking initiative for solving problems."* Depending on how you defined it within your *"2.5 Rule"* description of this behavior, this golden nugget could fit in several places within your organization's form—*"Description Of Performance," "Areas Of Strength,"* or in the *"Areas Of Needed Improvement"* section. Or, if your form has an *"Assessment Of Traits"* section, just transfer your *"2.5 Rule"* description next to the trait it best reflects *(e.g., "Initiative," "Problem Solving," etc.).*

Playing the numbers game

No book on performance evaluation is complete without a discussion about numerical ratings. This guidebook will only scratch the surface—run your complex questions and situations by your Human Resources professionals.

Often, employees complain that numerical rating systems are highly subjective. Consider Laurie Jean, an employee whose frustration with numerical ratings on performance evaluations is understandable:

"I work for one supervisor who gives me a '5' rating for my organizational skills. Then I get a new boss, and he gives my same performance a '3.' How can I be a '5' and a '3' at the same time?!"

Actually, she can. But given what little information she has to work with within her review—unsubstantiated numerical ratings, judgmental blurbs regarding her traits, etc.—her point of view is completely understandable. Were her supervisors' ratings and descriptions wrong? Yes and no.

When you interview the first supervisor, you learn that the organizational skills assessed as *"5–Outstanding"* were accurately referring to Laurie's performance while organizing projects. The second supervisor's rating of *"3–Acceptable/Meets Expectation"* accurately reflected Laurie's performance while organizing staff roles and responsibilities. In other words, Laurie's performance could be *"Unacceptable," "Meets Expectations,"* and *"Outstanding"* regarding organizational skills *at the same time,* depending on how the skills are defined. *(Look at the way you organize your thoughts, memos, meetings, desk drawers—even your closets at home!)*

Where the supervisors failed was in their communication and *"documentation"* of their expectations, priorities, and observations. They may have been clear verbally, but not on paper. Verbal descriptions last as long as memories; written descriptions last a bit longer. Learn to support all ratings with well-constructed descriptions of your team members' behavior following *"The 2.5 Rule."*

If your performance-evaluation form uses a numerical rating system, use it wisely. Based on most rating definitions, most of your team members' performance ratings will likely be *"Acceptable/ Meets Expectations"* or better *(or whatever rating your form has that is equivalent to the "middle" rating and above).*

Other points to consider when using a numerical rating system follow *(this is just the tip of the iceberg.):*

♦ Although you would not expect to see a team's ratings distributed as a *"perfect bell-shaped curve,"* normally fewer team members are rated above *"Acceptable/Meets Expectations"* *(i.e., "Very Good" or its equivalent),* and even fewer are rated at the highest level of the rating scale *(i.e., as "Outstanding" or its equivalent).* Use your best judgment. But what if you're surrounded by a bunch of superstars? The stronger you feel this way about your team members, the greater the likelihood you like, hired, and/or developed them. Run your drafts and ratings by an objective third party who may be familiar with the performance of your team *(e.g., customers, senior managers, Human Resources, etc.)* to ensure you're not guilty of rate inflation! An *"Acceptable/Meets Expectations"* rating *(often the midpoint of rating scales)* is not the same as a "C" in grade school! It should be used as often as necessary.

♦ Some team members may fall into the *"Needs Improvement"* category—this does not necessarily mean that they are poor performers. Often, it is common for team members to take on new and unfamiliar responsibilities in a growing organization. Explain your rating with a *"2.5 Rule"* description.

♦ If an overall performance rating is required, keep in mind that some factors may have more *"weight"* than others in influencing this overall rating. For example, if you rated a team member as a "3" on a "1-5" scale *("5" being highest)* for *"Team Playing"* and a rating of "5" for *"Self Directed,"* etc., your overall rating may not necessarily be an average of the two or more individual ratings. Case in point: If your team member is a successful salesperson who must work autonomously on the road, his overall rating may be better described with a "4.5" or higher *(even though the average rating for these two factors is "4"; "Self Directed" may deserve more "weight" given his job's requirements).*

Every organization that uses a numerical rating system will likely field complaints about *"hard graders"* or inconsistencies between departments regarding what is or isn't *"acceptable."* Minimize such complaints by making sure that the performance evaluation *(your solid research and "2.5 Rule" descriptions)* drives the performance ratings, and not vice versa! The *"scores"* you give to others are as much a reflection of you!

Alex Weiss is in upper management...

at a medium-sized manufacturing firm that produces medical equipment for the health industry. He now readily admits that his *"hands-off"* coaching style with respect to performance evaluations has not worked very well with two of the supervisors he oversees–Karen Davis and Arnold Blalock. He's been getting a mountain of complaints from their employees, and now wants to rectify the situation.

"The reason I wanted to talk to you both is because of inconsistencies in how you rate your people—inconsistencies that may come back to haunt us," Alex began. *"Karen, you have a tendency to rate members of your team higher than they may deserve. You gave Jay an 'Outstanding' in every area, including 'Attendance.' How can that be, when you've told me numerous times that his absenteeism has had a detrimental affect on the performance of your three-person team?"*

"Well, he gets the work out when he's here," Karen responded.

"But what about the impacts to your team when he's not?" Alex followed.

Arnold interrupted. *"You gave that slacker a '5' for 'Attendance!?'"* he said. *"You gotta be kidding me! If he was in my department, he would have earned a new rating— 'minus two!'"*

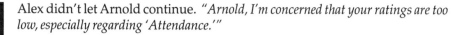

Alex didn't let Arnold continue. *"Arnold, I'm concerned that your ratings are too low, especially regarding 'Attendance.'"*

Arnold defended himself: *"I need them here or I don't meet production schedules."*

"Of course you have a legitimate concern," Alex began, *"but rating Ruth a 'Poor' on 'Attendance' because she took four company sick-leave days in a year may be a little harsh. Especially since you have a twenty-person team to cover for her—the impacts of her absenteeism are less serious than if she were part of a three-person team."*

Alex continued coaching both supervisors: *"The standards in your departments need to be clearly understood, realistic, and fair. If there are variations between your departments, there need to be bonafide job requirements to support why—otherwise, we'll strive for total consistency. What I'd like to do is to go over each of your performance expectations for your team members. Together we'll decide on criteria for assigning rating scores that's fair to all supervisors and employees."*

In the next chapter, you'll discover how to make each team member's performance evaluation expand from a description of the past to a prescription for the future.

CHAPTER FOUR WORKSHEET: DESCRIBING TEAM MEMBER PERFORMANCE

1. Apply *"The 2.5 Rule"* and describe at least two behaviors *(e.g., one "Area Of Strength" and one "Area Of Needed Improvement")* for one of your team members.

---

1. BEHAVIOR (*STRENGTH*)

2. IMPACTS

(.5) EXAMPLE(S)

---

1. BEHAVIOR (*AREA OF NEEDED IMPROVEMENT*)

2. IMPACTS

(.5) EXAMPLE(S)

---

2. How descriptive were you? Ask a colleague if what you wrote was specific and behavioral-based. In other words, did you use *"The Write Stuff"*?

_____

_____

_____

_____

_____

_____

_____

_____

_____

3. Look at your organization's performance evaluation. Decide where *(i.e., in which section of the form)* each one of the behaviors you described above would logically fit. If necessary, *"code"* the sections of your organization's form and your descriptions.

DEVELOP AND REVIEW

❸

DEVELOP AND REVIEW

TASKS

♦ **IDENTIFY OPPORTUNITIES FOR EMPLOYEE GROWTH**

♦ **DRAFT EMPLOYEE DEVELOPMENT PROFILES TO ENHANCE PERFORMANCE**

♦ **SEEK SUPPORT FROM YOUR ORGANIZATION**

You've probably heard it before: *"Your employees are your greatest assets."* You might even believe it. But capitalizing on those assets can be a challenge when compared to other development activities, like upgrading your computer software—where you just hit the *"install"* button and reboot!

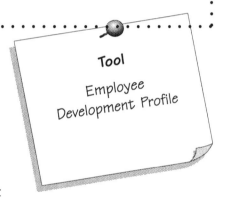

Tool

Employee Development Profile

Unfortunately, teams don't come with an owner's manual. One team member may be a self-starter—extremely motivated and sure of exactly what she wants. Just give her the tools she needs and get out of her way. Another may have a good sense of the skills he brings to the table, but is not clear how those skills can be best utilized or improved. You can help lead the way. Still another team member may be trying to answer the question, *"What am I doing here anyway?"* You could help open his eyes to see his current potential and future career opportunities *(or the door)*.

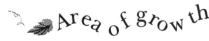

Area of growth

Thankfully, many people have an inner drive to improve or excel at something. It might be to speak a foreign language, give a persuasive presentation, develop a new computer program, run *(or finish)* a marathon, surf the Internet *(without drowning)*, break par on the golf course *(with a witness)*, or learn to skate backwards *(just don't ask why)*. Wouldn't it be something to harness that energy? You might actually see people having fun at work! It can happen if *(and this is a big IF)* you invest the time to jointly develop each of your team members while considering the needs of the team member, you, your team, and your organization.

Regardless of your team member's style, ambition, experience, etc., you have an opportunity to take this *"diamond" (rough or polished)* and increase its value. Recommended tasks follow.

Identify Opportunities For Employee Growth

There's a mindset that says, *"People should be responsible for their own development. After all, I did everything on my own."* The truth is, though, that no one does it alone. If you were honest, someone probably gave you some needed direction or resources at a crucial time in your career. This is where team leaders can make a big difference. Invest in your team members by developing them, and they will pay great dividends.

Where do you begin?

For each team member, consider identifying one to three *"Areas For Growth"* for the next review period. Choose strengths on which to capitalize *(leverage your assets)*, and/or *"Areas Of Needed Improvement"* on which to build further competencies or confidence. Select those that most directly affect on-the-job performance, and allow for improvement to be clearly prescribed and measured.

This part is relatively easy. Your choices will come *directly* from the team member's performance evaluation you've drafted so far. Remember *"The 2.5 Rule?"* You'll be choosing behaviors you described using it. Then, once you've chosen your team member's *"Areas For Growth,"* you'll be able to work with her to develop those areas. And there is a tool that will help you do this—the Employee Development Profile.

Draft Employee Development Profiles To Enhance Performance

At this point, you have identified one to three *"Areas For Growth"* for a team member to concentrate on during the next review period. Now you both need to determine *how* this team member can enhance an *"Area Of Needed Improvement,"* and/or capitalize on a performance strength using an Employee Development Profile *(EDP).*

The EDP not only assists team members in their current roles, it also can be used to help them acquire skills for new roles, responsibilities, projects, and opportunities. The EDP also substantially increases the chances of employee development taking place because you have a plan in writing. You and your team member both agree and commit to it.

The three steps involved in building an EDP follow.

BUILDING AN EMPLOYEE DEVELOPMENT PROFILE

Determining how to enhance a behavior (skill) following these three steps:

1. AREA FOR GROWTH

Describe a team member's selected skill or behavior to be developed—following *"The 2.5 Rule."* Choose an *"Area Of Strength"* on which to capitalize *(leverage your assets),* and/or an *"Area Of Needed Improvement"* on which to build further competencies or confidence.

2. DEVELOPMENT ACTIONS

List at least three to four ways to develop this *"Area For Growth."* Include specific examples of on- and off-the-job development actions and key milestone dates to review progress.

3. EXPECTED RESULTS

Identify what results you collectively expect—measurements with which to evaluate the team member's performance of each *"Development Action,"* and evaluation methods with which to collect, interpret, and describe performance data.

Your team members' EDPs are a perfect complement to their performance plans and Performance Progress Sheets *(see **Planning Successful Employee Performance** and **Coaching For Peak Employee Performance**).* You've evaluated your team members based on expectations clarified within their performance plans. You've described behaviors linked to your documentation—including Performance Progress Sheets—while coaching them. And now, in the EDPs, you're highlighting ways to develop selected *"Areas For Growth."* The EDP may also help you create new *(or revise current)* performance plans for the next review period. In other words, evaluating is easier if you did your work in planning and coaching. Planning and coaching for the next review period is easier if you do your work in evaluating!

Completing the Employee Development Profile

Although the Employee Development Profile is presented to you as a form, this supplemental worksheet is only a guide to help you in preparation for a more important discussion with your team member regarding developing selected skills. You don't need the form, but it could help both of you on an *"as needed"* basis *(and is available in the Appendix)*. Or, incorporate the key components of the EDP within any similar section of your organization's performance-evaluation form.

Begin drafting EDPs *(at least have the "2.5 Rule" descriptions of skills/ behaviors)* before you meet with your team members. Remember, you're not starting from scratch! You'll be selecting *"2.5 Rule"* descriptions of behaviors that you've already written. Then jot a few ideas down in each section. Invest about ten minutes. You're not writing a strategic plan. You're just collecting enough rough ideas to begin a discussion with your team members. It will also test how well you've done so far. Chances are, if you can't think of any *"Development Actions,"* it's because you haven't written a description of a behavior that meets *"The 2.5 Rule."*

The Appendix has a number of lists that will help you develop EDPs. Look at *"Choosing 'Development Actions'"* for a list of possible on- and off-the-job options; read through *"Clarifying 'Expected Results'"* for possible measurements and evaluation methods to determine what will give you the best return on your investment *(ROI)*; and read *"Understanding Why Employee Development Profiles Succeed Or Fail"* to help you create the best possible EDP.

Team members should complete a major portion of any EDP. *(The greater their participation, the greater their commitment to success.)* Team leaders should offer guidance. Team leaders may also have certain actions to perform to make the EDP possible to implement *(e.g., provide access to resources, funding, time, direct one-one-one coaching, etc.).*

If it's a simple EDP, it may be agreed upon during one meeting *(i.e., the same meeting as the one in which you discuss the team member's performance evaluation—see Chapter Six).* If it's a complex EDP, it may require several meetings to complete. *(Review and completion dates should be established during the performance-evaluation meeting.)*

If your team members desire to complete additional EDPs related to other performance strengths or weaknesses, encourage and support them to do this following your performance-evaluation process.

The following four examples of Employee Development Profiles can be used as references or models as you create your own EDPs for your team members.

EMPLOYEE DEVELOPMENT PROFILE

TEAM MEMBER:	TITLE:	ORIGINATED:
TEAM:	TEAM LEADER:	REVISED:

AREA FOR GROWTH (FOLLOWING "THE 2.5 RULE")	DEVELOPMENT ACTIONS	EXPECTED RESULTS
Example # 1 *(Area Of Needed Improvement)* 1. Chris reviews project progress with internal customers annually or upon their request.	A. List *(and schedule)* who to see and what to ask. Have the lists and schedule completed for review with manager by XX/XX/XX.	A. Thoroughness and accuracy of lists, etc., verified through manager feedback.
2. As a result, customers share little information with him or his team. Changes to customer requirements are discovered too late for his team to act upon, customer decisions are made that exclude his department, and opportunities to build customer relationships and trust are minimized.	B. Apply these lists, and provide a verbal summary from these customer meetings. Summaries should be provided to our project team during our Thursday 9:00 am meetings.	B. Thoroughness, on-time, customer perception that Chris is *"value-added"* and meets/ exceeds expectations, etc., verified through customer feedback from interviews, and feedback solicited from project team members.
	C. Complete a special assignment— a briefing of the findings for presentation at our senior staff meeting on XX/XX/XX.	C. Thoroughness of research and presentation, ability to field questions, etc., as verified through feedback solicited from senior management.
(.5) *(e.g., "XYZ" project with "ABC" internal customer.)*	D. Begin mentoring and modeling others' behavior by attending the next four meetings manager conducts with the customer. Take notes and debrief observations with manager. Manager will then observe four of Chris' meetings.	D. Ability to summarize key points, performance in relation to expected behaviors, models, etc., as verified through direct observations and coaching from manager.

EMPLOYEE DEVELOPMENT PROFILE

TEAM MEMBER:	TITLE:	ORIGINATED:
TEAM:	TEAM LEADER:	REVISED:

AREA FOR GROWTH (FOLLOWING "THE 2.5 RULE")	DEVELOPMENT ACTIONS	EXPECTED RESULTS
Example # 2 *(Area Of Strength)* **1.** Toni uses small group facilitation skills that encourage equal contribution in group decision making.	**A.** Continue to practice skills and act as a role model to other employees in our department staff meetings. Identify regular portions of our meetings where you can exhibit these leadership and facilitation skills to help us meet our objectives, and begin applying this process in our meeting on XX/XX/XX.	**A.** Others' eagerness to work with Toni, increase in demand for Toni as a facilitator and/or advisor, etc., as verified through feedback from peers.
	B. Volunteer to lead committee decision making. Identify one to two committee memberships to pursue by XX/XX/XX.	**B.** Achieving expected results from committee meetings, etc., as verified through feedback from participant interviews.
2. As a result, superior work is being delivered ahead of schedule, she maintains high team morale, and she enjoys free time to spend on other projects.	**C.** Identify a successful mentor *(to interview, observe, critique)* for manager approval by XX/XX/XX. Meet with him/her on a scheduled basis. Provide a verbal synopsis to manager of learning by XX/XX/XX.	**C.** Applicability of list of key factors and behaviors and to projects, appropriately applying skills observed, etc., as verified through direct observations from manager and feedback from interview with mentor.
(.5) *(e.g., encouraging participation through open-ended questions, and problem solving and brainstorming methods; resolving the "XYZ" problem.)*	**D.** Continue to participate in training programs to enhance skill base. Enroll in the "ABC" and "XYZ" training programs scheduled for XX/XX/XX.	**D.** Frequent and appropriate application of new skills learned, etc., as verified through feedback from Trainer and observations from manager.

EMPLOYEE DEVELOPMENT PROFILE

TEAM MEMBER:	TITLE:	ORIGINATED:
TEAM:	TEAM LEADER:	REVISED:

AREA FOR GROWTH (FOLLOWING "THE 2.5 RULE")	DEVELOPMENT ACTIONS	EXPECTED RESULTS
Example # 3 (Area Of Needed Improvement) 1. Pat handles all direct internal customer contact and tasks by herself versus delegating this responsibility to others with the appropriate skills and availability. 2. As a result, this prevents Pat from: taking on additional responsibilities and accomplishing more, fully recognizing and developing the department's talents and resources, and providing internal customers with different yet complementary perspectives. (.5) (e.g., "ABC" and "XYZ" customers, "TBD" and "FYI" projects)	**A.** Create an inventory of skills, abilities, and interests of staff, and a list of future projects for which each would be qualified. Complete and review the list/matrix with each employee and with manager by XX/XX/XX.	**A.** Thoroughness, accuracy, and useful-ness of the matrix of skills and development plans, realistic plans for using the tools, etc., as verified through feedback from manager.
	B. Conduct one-on-one coaching sessions with selected employees to provide them an appropriate "script" with which to lead meetings with customers (train on what to cover and how). Create and review the "script" with manager by XX/XX/XX, and conduct at least three coaching sessions with three different employees by XX/XX/XX.	**B.** Thoroughness and usefulness of the "script," creativity and leadership from Pat's staff, increased free time for Pat, Pat using an effective coaching style, etc., as verified through customer feedback from interviews, and feedback from Pat's employees and manager.
	C. Take selected employees to observe Pat's next few meetings with customers. Identify selected employees for manager approval, and schedule them to accom-pany Pat on at least two or three occasions before XX/XX/XX.	**C.** Perceptions that Pat is recommending trained staff as alternatives, other employees leading customer meetings effectively are seen as value-added and are requested for future projects, etc., as verified through customer feedback from interviews and feedback from manager.
	D. Delegate responsibilities of next study to a skilled employee, have them dry run a presentation, and offer direct coaching. Incorporate dry run presentations into our regular staff meetings and lead an open and objective critique of the employee's performance with staff by XX/XX/XX.	**D.** Effectiveness of dry run presentations, effective-ness of Pat's coaching, etc., as verified through feedback from Pat's employees.

EMPLOYEE DEVELOPMENT PROFILE		
TEAM MEMBER:	**TITLE:**	**ORIGINATED:**
TEAM:	**TEAM LEADER:**	**REVISED:**
AREA FOR GROWTH (FOLLOWING "THE 2.5 RULE")	**DEVELOPMENT ACTIONS**	**EXPECTED RESULTS**
Example # 4 *(Area Of Needed Improvement)* **1.** Sean is often the only active speaker and participant in department meetings he leads.	**A.** Identify an effective meeting facilitator (as a mentor) and schedule him/her to co-facilitate a department meeting before XX/XX/XX.	**A.** Discuss observations and learning experiences with mentor and manager, etc., and verify feedback from meeting participants.
2. As a result, Sean's input—although perceived as value-added—often dominates the discussion, and employees don't feel that their input and opinions are heard or respected. Eventually they cease contributing and merely wait for Sean's direction.	**B.** Assign other department employees responsibility to lead or facilitate department meetings on a rotational basis beginning XX/XX/XX.	**B.** Effectiveness of meetings per objectives, levels of participation, etc., as verified through Manager's observation of department staff meetings and feedback from department employees.
	C. Read and highlight a relevant book on meeting effectiveness (especially how to facilitate greater team participation) by XX/XX/XX.	**C.** Discuss highlights and recommendations with manager.
(.5) (e.g., "ABC" and "XYZ" meetings)	**D.** Research external training opportunities to identify appropriate seminar on facilitating effective team meetings and attend by XX/XX/XX.	**D.** Discuss training highlights and recommendations with manager. Apply in upcoming team meeting.

These examples of Employee Development Profiles *(EDPs)* may be more or less detailed than your own. Develop EDPs that meet the needs of your team members, you, and your organization. However, try to avoid the most common pitfalls:

Pitfall 1 Not following "The 2.5 Rule" when describing the behavior for the "Area For Growth"

You won't save time by not following *"The 2.5 Rule."* If you start with, *"Sarah is disorganized," "Nathaniel is rude,"* or *"Stuart is not a team player,"* you're not only judging the person *(expect a bad meeting coming to an office near you)*, but you'll find the *"Development Actions"* very difficult to prescribe. *"Nathaniel, don't be rude; be nice"* just won't cut it. If you're having trouble writing clear and objective descriptions of behavior, re-read Chapter Four.

Pitfall 2 Suggesting a "Development Action" that's not linked to any "Area For Growth"

The most common recommendation for employee development that inexperienced managers write on performance evaluations is *"Attend 'XYZ' training class."* Why blindly send your team members to training seminars each year hoping they'll get better? Better at what? Being gone from the job?

Training programs are effective resources for employee development. But before considering any *"Development Action"*— including training—for your team members, determine if the *"Development Action"* is directly related to a team member's *"Area Of Strength"* on which you're trying to capitalize, or an *"Area Of Needed Improvement"* you're trying to develop.

Additionally, don't spread your efforts too thin by trying to do too much with your team members. This isn't school. They already have a full plate of job responsibilities!

Pitfall 3 — Identifying only one "Development Action"

What if you only prescribe one *"Development Action?"* Think of any skill you've learned in your life. Did you acquire this competency or ability all at one time and in one way? Certainly not. Then why waste your and your team member's time trying to find the perfect fix? Only one remedy? One single answer?

Remember Duane in the last chapter? He was told to *"take a class to learn 'XYZ' spreadsheet software."* Again, training classes are excellent options to consider as you build a plan for learning. You gain new tools, insights, and skills. But they're designed to complement many other developmental activities.

What if Duane also worked with an expert as she converted his handwritten tables into spreadsheets with automated formulas? Cross-trained with a team member who uses the software for other applications? Or worked through a self-paced users manual? Maybe other spreadsheet software would be better than the *"XYZ"* brand. Or maybe Duane isn't the best candidate for the job—someone else should do it.

Identify **three or more** *"Development Actions"* to increase the odds of success. If a training class is an option, list it *fourth.* This will challenge you and your team member to come up with three more creative options. Everyone learns differently, some plans may not be that successful once they're implemented, etc.

You don't want to be talking with your team member about the same *"Area For Growth"* during the next performance evaluation, do you?

Pitfall 4   Not identifying "Expected Results" *(or identifying the wrong ones)*

This is like investing your money without knowing the expected return on your investment *(ROI)*. You may not get at all what you want, and you may even lose what you had! The more clearly you and your team members identify what *"success"* is, the greater the likelihood it will be achieved. There are many measurements and methods. Discussing these *"Expected Results"* will help you choose the ones that will give you both a greater ROI.

For example, when team leaders send others to training classes, what do you think is the most common measure used? Likely nothing or *"attendance"* *("Did you go?" "Yes." "How was it?" "Fine." "Great.")*. Instead, consider what would happen if the team leader and team member picked one of the following *"Expected Results"*:

♦ Ask the team member to pick one tool or technique learned in the class and apply it to resolve or improve a real business issue; then ask him to discuss the pros and cons with the team.

♦ Ask the team member to train your team on how to use one selected tool or technique in a meeting following the class.

♦ Assign a project to the team member that must be done using the new tools or techniques covered in the class; schedule him to attend the class—then ask him to complete the project accordingly and discuss results.

♦ Ask the team member to recommend other team members who should attend the class, identify which tools or techniques each could use on the job, and why; then have her present these proposals to the team.

Would one of these *"Expected Results"* have changed the ROI? Try them out. You be the judge!

Seek Support From Your Organization

After you've drafted your Employee Development Profiles, and completed your performance evaluations, you'll likely need to meet with several others—the next-level team leader, manager, Human Resources representative, etc.—to review your work and to seek approval of your documentation. You need their complete support. *(Some of these people were already "resources" you have tapped for performance input during your data-collection step.)* This is a wise practice for several additional reasons:

1. They may act as a neutral third party to help ensure your descriptions of performance are direct, non-judgmental, and appropriate. You may even want to *"role play"* with them *(i.e., have them act as though they're the team member being evaluated)* to give you practice conducting portions of the performance-evaluation meeting.

2. They may disagree with descriptions within your evaluation, and may even ask you to amend it. Don't disregard any disagreements. You may have to change wording to protect the employee, to better align with company policy, or to reduce legal risks. And, yes, you may be asked to change a few words based solely on your manager's preference. Unless your manager's revisions change the whole meaning of your description, try to live with them—the fact is that there are many ways to describe a behavior.

    If you feel strongly, however, that the recommended amendments will inappropriately change your description of performance, stand your ground. Explain *"The 2.5 Rule"* to your manager, share your intentions, and look for common ground—words you both can live with *(ask your manager to read Chapter Four).*

3. They may have knowledge of upcoming organizational changes, special assignments, project leadership opportunities, transfer or promotional possibilities, etc., that could directly affect you and your team member.

4. Finally, it's good management practice. Your effectiveness as a team leader is, to an extent, dependent on how closely you collaborate with your team members and with those in authority above you.

Having completed these tasks, you should congratulate yourself. The hard work is done. You and your team member are both well prepared to discuss your documentation. Guidelines for this final step will be reviewed next in Chapter Six.

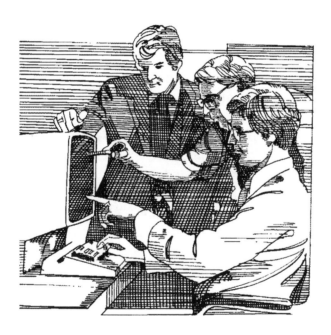

CHAPTER FIVE WORKSHEET:
PROFILING YOUR GREATEST ASSETS

1. Turn to the Appendix and copy and complete two Employee Development Profiles *(e.g., one for an "Area Of Strength" and one for an "Area Of Needed Improvement")* for one of your team members. Then, with the help of a colleague, critique your EDPs by answering the following questions.

2. Do your descriptions of the team member's *"Areas For Growth"* follow *"The 2.5 Rule"?*

    a. Was the behavior clearly described in succinct terms *(using at least one full sentence)*?

    b. Were the impacts of the behavior specifically explained *(using at least one full sentence)*?

    c. Were at least one or two specific and convincing examples cited of where this behavior was observed *(using one "half sentence—i.e., a phrase in parentheses)*?

    d. Is there a better way to describe each *"Area For Growth"* that is more succinct, more specific, clearer, etc.? If so, how?

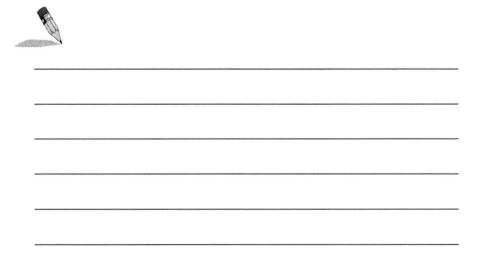

_____

_____

_____

_____

_____

_____

3. Does each *"Development Action"* and related *"Expected Results"* meet the following tests?

a. Is each *"Development Action"* directly related to the *"Area For Growth"*?

b. Is each action and result clear and specific (*i.e., Would this team member know exactly what to do and how he is going to be evaluated*)? If not, what is a better way to be more succinct, more specific, clearer, etc.?

_____

_____

_____

_____

c. If this team member performs all *"Development Actions"* listed and meets all *"Expected Results,"* will the *"Area For Growth"* be completely addressed (*i.e., Would you be completely satisfied that this "Area Of Strength" is "fully leveraged," or that this "Area Of Needed Improvement" is no longer a weakness*)? If not, what other *"Development Actions"* and/or *"Expected Results"* could be prescribed to assist this team member?

_____

_____

_____

_____

CONDUCT AND SUMMARIZE

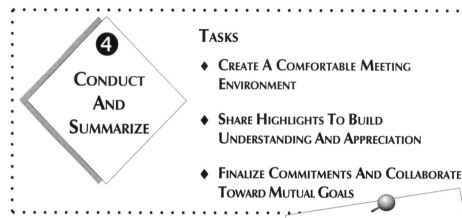

TASKS

♦ **CREATE A COMFORTABLE MEETING ENVIRONMENT**

♦ **SHARE HIGHLIGHTS TO BUILD UNDERSTANDING AND APPRECIATION**

♦ **FINALIZE COMMITMENTS AND COLLABORATE TOWARD MUTUAL GOALS**

Tool

Your organization's performance-evaluation form

Now you can finally reap the fruits of all of your efforts. Your reward is a productive and focused performance-evaluation meeting, because both you and your team member are properly prepared. What's left are just a few ideas and suggestions for making your performance-evaluation meetings as successful as possible.

Create A Comfortable Meeting Environment

Before the performance-evaluation meeting, increase the likelihood of success by creating the right atmosphere. Consider the following:

1. **Reserve a comfortable, neutral, and private place to meet.**

   The meeting environment should make your team members comfortable—encouraging equal and open participation. Therefore, avoid places that can be intimidating, like your office—with you behind a large desk and your team member facing you (*awaiting "judgment day"*), feeling very exposed and subordinate.

Consider a neutral site, perhaps a conference room with a round table. If the table is square, position the chairs at adjoining *(versus opposing)* sides. This will encourage an atmosphere of collaboration, rather than confrontation. Ensure that this physical space is private and free from outside distraction. Make arrangements to hold interruptions, including visitors and phone calls. That pretty much rules out an open cubicle *(without a door)* or the company cafeteria.

2. Set aside sufficient time.

This meeting should take place at least annually. And you, your team member, and many others have invested some quality time to prepare for it. So, why rush? It's better to schedule more time than you think you'll need. At minimum, an hour or two. Maybe several meetings. Since performance evaluation is a process, not an event, don't feel it all has to happen at one time.

3. Give the employee ample notice.

If you followed the guidelines within Chapter Three, your team members have already been highly involved. Just give them plenty of notice regarding the meeting times and places, what they need to bring, etc., so they can make the necessary arrangements.

4. Gather all the documentation you'll need.

Bring specific examples *(ideas and hard copies of forms, letters, reports, etc.)* to support what you're going to say. The examples you need to be familiar with are *"built in"* to your *"2.5 Rule"* descriptions of behaviors! Make a copy of the performance-evaluation form itself so that the employee can comfortably refer to it as your discussion progresses.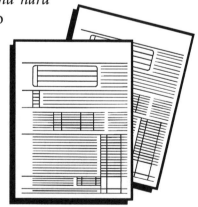

5. Plan opening remarks.

Yes, some people can *"wing it"*—but many can't. Think about how you want to open the meeting. Maybe you want to thank your team member for all of his efforts so far, or let him know this is not an event, but a process. Consider providing a general overview of how you think the discussion time should be spent. You don't need to be too formal, just respectful of each other's time. A simple verbal agenda *(a mental map)* will work.

For example:

> Instead of reading through this form starting on page one, how about if we openly discuss the highlights of your past performance first? As we go, I'll pause us to show you how I've captured these thoughts in writing throughout this document. And then we can review the evaluation to cover those areas that did not spontaneously come up.

6. Prepare stimulating open-ended questions.

For many people, *"participation"* in their performance-evaluation meeting involves two words: *"Sign here."*

Here's an alternative: Treat the performance-evaluation meeting like you would an employment interview. Think about it. Interviewers ask questions to get candidates to do most of the talking. And instead of wasting both parties' time with, *"Tell me about yourself,"* professional interviewers prepare specific open-ended questions that gather pertinent information about relevant skills, knowledge, abilities, and experiences.

Therefore, to get your team members to do most of the talking during their performance evaluations, and to ensure their input will help your discussions *(versus just fill time)*, develop stimulating open-ended questions that will solicit information already documented within each section of the performance-evaluation form.

For example, you may choose to ask:

> During the past review period, what accomplishments were you most pleased with and why?

As the team member answers this question, have her pause so you can show how your written documentation reflects her verbal review. You may need to go to several sections of your organization's form to do this.

Examples of other stimulating questions include:

> If you could turn the clock back and do something differently, what would you do?

> What did you feel uncomfortable doing, due to a lack of experience, tools, support, time, etc.?

> How did you 'add value' to our team, project, organization, etc.?

> What project did you find most challenging, and why?

7. Start the meeting on time.

Although there are many understandable reasons why meetings start late, there are as many negative messages that this practice sends to your team members. If your employees are truly your greatest assets, then treat them with the greatest respect.

Share Highlights To Build Understanding And Appreciation

During the performance-evaluation meeting, seek to build understanding and appreciation of your team member's performance over the past review period. Focus your attention on your team member, not the form. And avoid *(like the plague)* reading the performance-evaluation form to your team member.

Give your team member a copy of the performance-evaluation form, and consider the following:

1. Use questions to direct your review of performance highlights.

Remember, it's not your performance evaluation you're conducting. Let your team member do most of the talking. Set a personal goal to have him talk at least 50 percent of the total time. Your stimulating open-ended questions *(prepared in advance)* will solicit his verbal self-assessment.

Use your questions. As your team member answers each, show him how you've highlighted his thoughts within your written documentation. In most cases, you will find yourself confirming what he's said or adding to his examples with your written comments.

2. Reinforce similarities in descriptions.

Using your written descriptions, occasionally pause your team member and paraphrase what you're hearing him say *(e.g., "I observed the same thing. As I summarized in this section of our form, I wrote...")* To do this, you must be very familiar with what you wrote and must listen intently to what you're hearing. Open your ears. When in doubt, probe for more information *(e.g., "Can you give me an example?" "What happened then?" etc.).* Keep your team member talking and keep listening!

3. Resolve differences in word choice.

If you have closely worked with your team members during the Planning and Coaching Phases, have closely involved them in the preparation of their evaluations, have closely followed the guidelines for *"The Write Stuff"* and *"The 2.5 Rule"* as you drafted their performance evaluations, etc., etc., etc., you've significantly reduced the likelihood of a problem with words on paper.

Inexperienced managers run into snags here, because they've done little to none of this. They surprise their team members with negative feedback never discussed before, they label their team members with judgments now forever documented in black and white, and they check boxes on rating scales without supporting their assessments with descriptions or examples. These team leaders are their own biggest problems!

Assumably, you're not one of them, so move on.

Rarely will your team members use the same words to describe their behaviors as those you chose to use when writing your descriptions. So don't dwell on the differences in word choice. Focus on the similarities in the *meanings* of your descriptions.

If a team member has a problem with a word you've chosen, discuss it now. Most of the time, she will *"live with"* your written descriptions (*just as you have accepted other word choices potentially "imposed" by your manager, Human Resources representative, etc., during the review of your draft*). Clearly explain that you're seeking her acceptance of your descriptions—she doesn't have to love every word. If this doesn't work, you basically have two options:

a. If possible, change a few words to satisfy your team member. Maybe her words *are* better. Avoid being the arrogant authoritarian. As long as you both agree on the *meaning*, and your original meaning doesn't change when a few words are changed, who cares whose words are chosen?

b. If this is not possible, or if you are positive that her suggested words would significantly alter the meaning of your description to a point where you can't accept it as accurate and objective, then encourage her to write her comments as a supplement to her performance evaluation. Most forms have an *"Employee Comments"* section, and most processes have an *"employee rebuttal or grievance"* procedure. Just ensure that this is the last resort, since it rarely will enhance your working relationship!

4. Share descriptions not yet covered.

As you prompt your team member for information, and connect his comments to your written evaluation, you'll find you have little left undisclosed to actually read to him. (*This should encourage you to prepare more and better questions—it'll make both of your jobs much easier and more enjoyable!*)

Walk him through those sections of the form that his answers didn't touch upon. Solicit his thoughts and support. He may be more quiet during this stage, but that's okay. Remember that this is a process, not a one-shot deal. He has a copy of the form and can read and discuss it with you later, too!

Finalize Commitments And Collaborate Toward Mutual Goals

Toward the end of *(and after)* the performance-evaluation meeting, set the stage for potential next steps. You'll need to:

1. **Finalize Employee Development Profiles.**

   As explained in Chapter Five, your drafts of Employee Development Profiles need to be finalized with your team members. Start that process now, and continue your discussions in subsequent meetings. Give your team members all of your notes. Some will have ideas now and want closure before they end this meeting. Others will want to *"sleep on it"* and get back to you.

   The EDPs are for your team members' development—let them make the call, but don't let them drop the ball. Be willing to review alternative plans for getting results. Finalize and document all key *"Development Actions"* and *"Expected Results"* and check for understanding with your team members.

2. **Discuss performance plans and career aspirations.**

   Allow some time during the performance-evaluation meeting for your team members to begin to share their thoughts about their current roles and responsibilities, as well as their career aspirations. They may want to get involved in other projects, negotiate changes in their responsibilities, clarify future performance expectations, get help with their next career steps, or acquire some new skills.

If you feel you can offer them some general direction or suggestions now, do so. But avoid making any promises as to available project assignments, job openings, etc. Wait until you are sure you can follow-through.

You're better off just listening and taking notes. Recommend that a separate meeting be scheduled in the near future to continue this conversation. That way you can give the topic the attention it deserves.

At this next meeting, you can discuss current performance plans *(Position Descriptions, Performance Objectives, and Performance Action Plans)*, and determine if any changes are necessary for the coming year. *(See **Planning Successful Employee Performance** for ideas on how to do this.)* You could also identify internal and external resources to assist your team members with career development, and to help them objectively assess their interests, potential, and opportunities.

3. **Secure your team member's acceptance.**

There is no rule, law, or policy that says your team member has to sign the performance-evaluation form at the end of this meeting. Some employees will be more comfortable if they have a chance to read it over and get it back to you within a few hours, a day, or more. Be sensitive to their needs and encourage them to make the call. Just let them know when you need it.

Do explain that signatures only historically document for the organization that performance evaluations have been discussed and that they have received their copy. Remember, you're seeking your team members' acceptance, not necessarily their complete agreement—although that would be great!

If a team member refuses to sign, explain again the meaning of her signature and other recourses she has *(including adding comments, a formal rebuttal, and/or an appeal to the next level of management or Human Resources; see #3 in the previous section— "Resolve Differences In Word Choice")*. Share that, much like receiving a speeding ticket from a police officer, she doesn't have to agree. Options are available. A signature only indicates receipt.

If she still refuses to sign, write or type the following directly on her signature line *"Employee refuses to sign"*—and any other documentation of explanations and help you offered. Do not leave the signature line blank. Memories fade faster than documents. Then review what happened with Human Resources and the next level of management.

Assuming most of the above doesn't happen to you, close the meeting on a positive note. Assure the team member of your willingness to talk further at a later date, if he has any additional questions or suggestions. Begin to recognize and reward efforts toward mutual goals.

The next chapter is for those team leaders who, in spite of all their planning and coaching, still have employees with performance problems. Corrective action, a proven method *(and last resort)* can help redirect employees with challenging behaviors while protecting you and your organization.

CHAPTER SIX WORKSHEET: PREPARING FOR THE PERFORMANCE-EVALUATION MEETING

1. List at least ten stimulating open-ended questions that you will ask your team member during an upcoming performance-evaluation meeting. Develop questions that will solicit information you've already documented within each section of your organization's performance-evaluation form.

_____

_____

_____

_____

_____

_____

_____

_____

_____

_____

_____

_____

_____

_____

2. Anticipate what your team member's answers might be to the previous questions during the performance-evaluation meeting. How will you respond? What follow-up questions could you ask?

_____

_____

_____

_____

_____

_____

_____

_____

_____

_____

_____

_____

_____

_____

_____

_____

_____

_____

3. Critically evaluate the last performance evaluation you had with a team member. What worked well? What could be improved? What will you do differently next time? Develop an action plan below, after considering some of the suggestions within this chapter.

_____

_____

_____

_____

_____

_____

_____

_____

_____

_____

_____

_____

_____

_____

_____

_____

CORRECTIVE ACTIONS

Nine times *(or more)* out of ten, you will be dealing with winning team members. They might not all be peak performers, but they're performing at their best potential and meeting your expectations. For this *"exceptional majority,"* your responsibility as their team leader will be to continually find creative ways to recognize, reward, and motivate them. *(Refer to* **Coaching For Peak Employee Performance** *for many ideas to help you get started. It will also help you coach the "marginal" or "below average" performers who require much of a manager's time and patience.)*

This chapter will help you document the performance of the remaining few team members who—even after repeated coaching sessions, development efforts, and performance evaluations—*still* don't meet your expectations.

Performance problems exist for a number of reasons. Some are work-related and some are not. Some are legitimate and some are not. To remain sane, keep your focus on on-the-job employee performance. If you can describe your team member's current behavior, and you have discussed and documented what the expected behavior should be, you're halfway to correcting the problem.

Of course, you still need the cooperation of your employee. One way of getting it is to take corrective action with progressive performance counseling.

Administer Progressive Performance Counseling

Progressive performance counseling—or discipline—is best administered when all other measures to assist an employee to meet his objectives and your expectations have failed.

Although the word *"discipline"* often carries a negative connotation, it comes from the verb *"disciple,"* which refers to teaching, training, and molding! Good discipline describes the condition that exists when *"the rules of the game"* are fair, consistent, understood, and followed. Fortunately, most people recognize that discipline is necessary and prefer to work under orderly and reasonable *"rules."* They like to know precisely where they stand and what is expected.

Others, however, need more direct help to accept that they have an *"Area Of Needed Improvement"* that's critical to address. Before taking these few team members through the steps of progressive performance counseling, you must be confident that you have considered the following:

BEFORE YOU "DISCIPLINE," HAVE YOU...

YES NO
- ☐ ☐ 1. Clearly instructed your team members on performance plans and expectations?
- ☐ ☐ 2. Observed their performance?
- ☐ ☐ 3. Provided feedback that performance did not meet plans and expectations?
- ☐ ☐ 4. Listened and responded to their concerns?
- ☐ ☐ 5. Assisted them with directions and resources?
- ☐ ☐ 6. Reinforced desirable behaviors?

If the answer is *"yes"* to all of these statements, and the employee *still* fails to meet agreed-upon standards, move forward to seek a second opinion (*e.g., from Human Resources*) to ensure that your pending corrective action with this employee is based on a *"sound business need."*

Together, review the checklist that follows (*and read "Adhering To Legal Accountabilities" in the Appendix*).

IS PROGRESSIVE PERFORMANCE COUNSELING APPROPRIATE?

YES   NO

❑   ❑   1. Does the unmet objective negatively affect the effectiveness and efficiency of operations?

❑   ❑   2. Is the employee fully aware, capable, and trained to meet the objective?

❑   ❑   3. Is the employee fully aware of the consequences for not meeting the objective?

❑   ❑   4. Is the consequence reasonably related to the seriousness of the unmet objective, and the employee's past track record?

❑   ❑   5. Do you have clear, objective, and substantial information that factually supports that the employee has not met the objective?

❑   ❑   6. Will you be treating this employee equitably and consistently in comparison to other employees under similar circumstances?

❑   ❑   7. Have you discussed your approach with the appropriate parties in your organization (*e.g., senior management, Human Resources, etc.*) prior to contacting the employee?

Corrective action must be uniform and progressive, so that all employees in an organization know what to expect. Consequences for repeated undesirable behaviors should be, step-by-step, more severe. For example, one manager should not give a verbal warning for an unexcused absence, while another discharges an employee for the same offense under the same circumstances.

Standard policies, procedures, and performance expectations should reduce such inequities. They also help to promote a reasonable and fair organization. When your employees know what is expected of them, they will most likely not feel threatened and may very well learn to discipline themselves!

Consider A Standard Process For Corrective Action

Following is a standard progressive performance-counseling *(progressive disciplinary)* process. Your organization's process for taking corrective action may vary. So may the steps you take. Some steps may be skipped based on the severity of the employee's behavior *(e.g., if an employee is suspected of stealing, most organizations will start at Step 4 or 5!).*

Know what disciplinary process your organization has in place; then consider the following steps:

Step 1: Verbal counseling

First, describe the *"Area(s) Of Needed Improvement"*—what your team member is doing, the undesirable impacts from his behavior, and examples—all, of course, following *"The 2.5 Rule"* *(see Chapter Four).*

Next, discuss alternative behaviors for the employee, you, and theirs to take to redirect his current behavior and reach desirable results *(expectations).* In many cases, your discussion will model the Employee Development Profile *(see Chapter Five)* as you build a common development plan to resolve the problems.

Solicit and respond to your team member's concerns and suggestions. Remember to avoid judgmental language *(see "The Write Stuff" in Chapter Four)* and arguments over word choices *(see Chapter Six).*

Last, summarize key steps for you and your team member to take, and schedule a review session. Note the dates, times, and key discussion points of this meeting in your own file. Offer a copy of your notes to the employee.

✔ Step 2: Verbal warning

Follow *all* of the suggestions in Step 1 above. Then, inform the team member that due to repeated undesirable behavior, this discussion *is* a verbal warning, and that more severe consequences will follow if immediate and measurable improvement is not observed.

Ask the employee for any reasons for the lack of behavioral change. You may get legitimate concerns (*e.g., computer-systems problems*), and/or an ear-full of gripes (*e.g., "It's not my fault"*). Rather than argue, do everything in your power to identify and remove all obstacles to expected performance. Take away all excuses.

Note the dates, times, and key discussion points of this meeting in your own file. Again, offer a copy of your notes to the team member (*you have no secrets*). Give a verbal update to the next level of management and Human Resources.

✔ Step 3: Written reprimand

Your verbal and written communications should mirror one another. The performance evaluations you write (*including "Written Reprimands"*) should have "*2.5 Rule*" descriptions of team members' behaviors that are, in essence, written summaries of discussions you've already had with them throughout the review period. The plans and agreements you document should model your verbal commitments to resolve performance issues to date. There should be no surprises.

Follow *all* of the suggestions in Steps 1 and 2. Then, develop a written reprimand with the assistance of the next level of management and Human Resources. Include the following points:

COMPONENTS OF A "WRITTEN REPRIMAND"

a. The purpose of the written reprimand—to improve behavior.

b. The "2.5 Rule" description of the "Area(s) Of Needed Improvement." Remember that this is a minimum writing rule. Write as many sentences as necessary to clearly document the problem behaviors, undesirable impacts *(especially the negative effects on business operations)*, and examples.

c. A reference to all previous verbal counseling and verbal warnings, including the dates, times, and key discussion points.

d. A statement of policy or customary practices regarding this situation. Demonstrate that you are treating this team member equitably and consistently.

e. A complete description of the required corrective actions, and time period for employee to demonstrate improvement. Include all resources and assistance provided by you and the organization.

f. A clear indication of the consequences of failure to improve (e.g., "...will immediately lead to further disciplinary action up to and including termination of employment").

g. Signature lines for all to sign. The employee's signature indicates that the written reprimand has been reviewed with her and she has been given a copy.

Then, meet with the team member to review the document. *(On occasion, it will be advantageous to have another member of management or a Human Resources representative present during the meeting, as a "witness" and to ensure all key points are covered.)* Inform the employee that due to repeated undesirable behavior, a written reprimand will now be used to help redirect his behavior. Give him a copy, and read through each and every paragraph. *(Note: This is intentionally a formal process and completely different than what was recommended in Chapter Six).* Respond to any questions your team member may have *(he'll likely have few).*

Ask your employee to sign the document. *(Refusal by an employee to sign the written reprimand in no way affects the force and effect of the reprimand. In this case, note "Refused to Sign" on the form, and have it witnessed.)* Then forward the document to the team member's personnel file.

This likely will not be a long meeting. You've discussed everything at length before. But don't forget the purpose of this meeting. You not only are trying to improve your team member's performance, you're also developing the written reprimand to protect you and your organization from a wrongful termination suit in the event you must terminate this employee. Yes, it would be great if the employee *"wows"* you with a complete turnaround in performance. Hope for it. But the odds are she'll begin looking for another job. That's why written reprimands—and progressive performance counseling—should be the last resort.

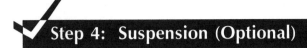
Step 4: Suspension (Optional)

Following a lack of improvement and/or serious allegations *(e.g., accusations of theft)*, the employee may be suspended from work with or without pay as a disciplinary action, to allow for further investigation. This step is usually approved by Human Resources in advance, and involves organization-specific steps, considerations, and forms.

Step 5: Termination

Always consult with senior management, Human Resources, and legal counsel before proceeding with a termination of employment. Again, your organization will have specific steps, considerations, and forms. Follow them.

You may never need to use the information in this chapter. However, for that one time you do, it'll be more than helpful. After all, being prepared is what successful performance evaluation is all about.

CHAPTER SEVEN WORKSHEET:
TAKING CORRECTIVE ACTIONS

1. For the 90 percent or more of your team members who are performing to your expectations, list several ways you could recognize, reward, and motivate them.

2. Consider an employee whose performance is currently below standards. Describe this team member's behavior following *"The 2.5 Rule" (from Chapter Four).* Then, describe what his or her behavior should be to meet expectations.

_____

_____

_____

_____

_____

_____

_____

_____

_____

_____

_____

_____

_____

_____

_____

_____

_____

3. Does your organization have a policy or procedure for progressive discipline? If so, what are the steps involved? Who do you contact for help in the event you need to take corrective action with an employee?

_____

_____

_____

_____

_____

_____

_____

_____

_____

_____

_____

_____

_____

_____

_____

_____

_____

CHAPTER EIGHT

SUMMARY

Congratulations! You are now a member of an exclusive group of leaders who, rather than treat performance evaluations as a bureaucratic waste of time, know how to use them as a valuable tool for documenting and developing their team members' performance. Now begin to help others to understand that:

Performance Evaluation Is...

♦ An ongoing, interactive process, not a form or an annual meeting

♦ Focused consistently and objectively on performance behaviors, not the person

♦ Inclusive of complete descriptions of performance and skills, explaining impacts to the business, and referencing examples

♦ A shared and participative process of documenting past performance and exploring future potential

♦ A helpful and necessary tool to reinforce or redirect performance

♦ Supported by solid research that legally defends personnel decisions

♦ An essential part of the Performance Management Cycle— planning, coaching, and *evaluating* employee performance

---

Continue to practice the skills you've learned. Share a few tools in this guidebook with someone else *(like your boss),* and make his or her life a little easier—and *your* performance evaluation a little better!

REFERENCE MATERIAL AND REPRODUCIBLE FORMS

Reference Material

Reproducible Forms*

*Note: The Reproducible Forms in the Appendix are provided for you to
copy and use appropriately.

APPENDIX

DESCRIBING SKILLS AND TRAITS

Sometimes, we all could use a little help trying to come up with the right words! The following lists of *"generic"* skills, and *"positive"* and *"negative"* traits may help.

Caution: No single word below is enough to describe your team member's performance. Use these words as *"kick starts"* for your Performance Evaluation Thought Jogger. Picture in your mind the team member you are evaluating, then *"run"* your eyes down the columns of words, and write the words that describe this employee on your Performance Evaluation Thought Jogger. Then expand each word into full descriptions of your team member's behaviors following *"The 2.5 Rule."*

"GENERIC" SKILLS

accept	complete	establish	interact	prepare	service
accomplish	comply	estimate	interpret	present	serve
acknowledge	compose	evaluate	interview	price	share
adjust	compromise	expedite	inventory	prioritize	solve
adhere	conceive	experiment	invoice	process	speak
advise	condense	explain	keep	program	staff
agree	conduct	extrapolate	lead	project	stimulate
allocate	confront	facilitate	learn	promote	summarize
analyze	consolidate	focus	leverage	propose	support
anticipate	consult	follow	listen	provide	talk
apply	control	forecast	maintain	publish	take
assemble	cooperate	formulate	manage	read	teach
assess	counsel	gather	mediate	reassure	team-play
assist	create	design	meet	recognize	test
assure	deal	guide	mentor	recommend	time
attend	decide	help	model	record	track
audit	define	hire	monitor	report	train
budget	delineate	identify	motivate	recruit	translate
building	deliver	implement	negotiate	repair	understand
chair	describe	incorporate	network	research	update
challenge	develop	influence	offer	resolve	use
change	direct	inform	operate	respond	validate
clarify	discuss	initiate	order	restate	write
coach	disseminate	innovate	organize	review	
collaborate	draft	inquire	orient	revise	
collect	draw	inspect	participate	reward	
communicate	edit	inspire	persuade	schedule	
compensate	encourage	install	place	select	
compile	ensure	instruct	plan	sell	

106

EVALUATING EMPLOYEE PERFORMANCE

"POSITIVE" TRAITS

accurate
active
adaptable
adventurous
alert
ambitious
appreciative
approachable
artistic
assertive
calm
capable
cautious
charming
cheerful
clear-thinking
clever
collaborating
competent
confident
conscientious
considerate
controlled
conversational
cooperative
courageous
creative
credible
curious
decisive
deliberate
democratic
dependable
detail-oriented
determined
dignified
diplomatic
direct
discreet
easy-going
effective
efficient
energetic

enterprising
enthusiastic
fair-minded
foresighted
formal
frank
friendly
generous
gentle
good-natured
healthy
helpful
honest
humorous
idealistic
imaginative
independent
individualistic
industrious
ingenious
initiating
innovative
influential
insightful
inspiring
intelligent
inventive
kind
knowledgeable
logical
loyal
mannerly
mature
methodical
moderate
motivational
natural
objective
open-minded
optimistic
organized
original
outgoing

outspoken
participative
patient
persevering
persistent
persuasive
planful
pleasant
poised
polished
popular
positive
practical
praising
pragmatic
precise
procedure-
oriented
professional
progressive
qualified
quick
rational
realistic
reasonable
reflective
relaxed
reliable
reserved
resourceful
responsible
results-
oriented
self-confident
sensitive
serious
sharp-witted
sincere
sociable
sophisticated
spontaneous
stable
steady

successful
sympathetic
systematic
tactful
talkative
team-oriented
thorough
thoughtful
thrifty
tolerant
trusting
trustworthy
unaffected
unassuming
unconventional
understanding
unselfish
versatile
warm
willing
wise
witty
yielding

"NEGATIVE" TRAITS

accusing
aggressive
aimless
alarmist
ambiguous
antagonistic
anxious
apathetic
apologetic
apprehensive
argumentative
authoritative
autocratic
bad-tempered
belittling
belligerent
biased
bitter
blunt
boisterous
busybody
careless
chaotic
challenging
childish
coercive
concealing
conformist
confrontational
conniving
contrary
controlling
controversial
critical
cynical
deceitful
defiant
deficient
dependent
detached

devious
dictatorial
disagreeable
discourteous
disillusioned
disliked
disorderly
disrespectful
dissatisfied
distrustful
dogmatic
domineering
doubtful
egotistical
emotional
envious
excitable
explosive
extravagant
extremist
farfetched
fatalistic
fault-finding
fearful
flamboyant
flippant
frantic
frustrated
fussy
gambler
gloating
hair-splitting
harassing
hasty
hostile
hurtful
hypocritical
ignorant
ill-mannered
ill-natured
immature
impatient

impressionable
impulsive
inaccessible
inactive
inadequate
inappropriate
inattentive
incompetent
inconsistent
indecisive
ineffectual
inefficient
inflexible
insensitive
intolerant
intimidating
irrational
irregular
jealous
late
lax
lethargic
malicious
mediocre
misconception
misrepresent
misunder-
standing
monotonous
narrow
negative
negligent
nervous
nontrusting
oblivious
obnoxious
obstructive
one-sided
overbearing
overpowering
overworked
partial

passive
pessimist
picayune
pompous
possessive
powerless
preoccupied
pretentious
procrastinator
quiet
rash
rebellious
reckless
relentless
remote
restless
rude
ruthless
seclusive
selfish
shaky
short-sighted
silent
slow
somber
spiteful
static
strained
stressed
stubborn
submissive
sulky
superficial
susceptible
suspicious
thoughtless
timid
tough
tricky
turbulent

unambitious
unapproachable
unaware
uncomfortable
uncommunicative
undignified
uneven
unfamiliar
unfavorable
unfocused
unforgiving
unfortunate
unhappy
unjustifiable
unkind
unmindful
unmotivated
unnecessary
unorganized
unpopular
unprepared
unproductive
unreliable
unsatisfactory
unskilled
unsteady
unsystematic
untrained
unwilling
vague
verbose
victim
wasteful
weak
withdrawn
withholding

AVOIDING MISUNDERSTANDINGS WHEN DESCRIBING SKILLS AND TRAITS

If your organization's performance-evaluation form has a section for you to assess your team members' skills and traits, appropriately supplement your numerical or scale ratings with clear descriptions following *"The 2.5 Rule."* If you don't, your evaluations may be no more than a bad joke that leads to misunderstandings.

	QUALITY OF WORK	PROMPTNESS	INITIATIVE	ADAPTABILITY	COMMUNICATION
Far Exceeds Job Requirements	Leaps tall buildings with a single bound.	Is faster than a speeding bullet.	Is stronger than a locomotive.	Walks on water.	Talks with you.
Exceeds Job Requirements	Leaps tall buildings with a running start.	Is as fast as a speeding bullet.	Is as strong as a bull elephant.	Keeps head above water under stress.	Talks with others.
Meets Job Requirements	Can leap short buildings if prodded.	Would you believe a slow bullet?	Almost as strong as a bull.	Washes with water.	Talks to themselves.
Needs Improvement	Bumps into buildings.	Misfires frequently.	Shoots the bull.	Drinks water.	Argues with themselves.
Does Not Meet Minimum Requirements	Cannot recognize buildings.	Wounds themselves when handling guns.	Smells like a bull.	Passes water in emergencies.	Loses arguments with themselves.

CHOOSING
"DEVELOPMENT ACTIONS"

Once you have selected your team member's *"Area(s) Of Strength"* and/or *"Area(s) Of Needed Improvement"* as *"Areas For Growth,"* you should establish an initial Employee Development Profile that describes how your team member will further enhance his/her performance in this area.

The following list may help you think of some directions and/or plans:

DEVELOPMENT ACTION	EXPLANATION
1. Job enrichment	Delegate more authority, autonomy, or ability to take more risks in the employee's current role *(e.g., more involvement in meetings representing their team).*
2. Job enlargement	Assign additional responsibilities to broaden the employee's current role.
3. On-the-job coaching	Impart skills, knowledge, and direction to develop the employee's insights and abilities to handle projects and problems by themselves the next time.
4. Special assignments	Provide opportunities for comprehensive research of a problem to enhance the employee's technical, analytical, and decision-making skills.
5. Job rotation or transfer	Move employee from one job to another to broaden his/her knowledge, experience, or perspective.

Development Action	Explanation
6. **Substitute assignment**	Assign the employee to temporarily assume the duties of another employee *(like you)* who is on vacation, traveling, on leave of absence, etc.
7. **Understudy**	Have the employee work directly with another to eventually assume responsibilities as a replacement.
8. **Mentorship**	Have the employee periodically *"interview"* a specialist to discuss and enhance business acumen.
9. **Leadership opportunity** *(internal/external)*	Have the employee lead meetings, presentations, task forces, etc., to enhance his/her knowledge, experience, and assume leadership responsibility in professional associations, conferences, etc., and/or community and employee involvement programs.
10. **Training assignment or presentation**	Arrange for the employee to cross-train others or present ideas, plans, findings, etc., to build knowledge, credibility, and confidence.
11. **Study materials**	Provide manuals, books, reports, tapes, cassettes, and other self-study reference materials. Follow-up to share interests and reinforce learning.
12. **Professional development programs**	Have the employee attend in-house and external workshops, conferences, and academic programs to develop specific skills and networks.

CLARIFYING "EXPECTED RESULTS"

To ensure you and your team members get the greatest return on your investments in Employee Development Profiles, clarify up-front what *"Expected Results"* are desirable—how will *"success"* be measured? Identify measurements and evaluation methods.

MEASUREMENTS

Agree upon specific ways you and your team member will measure and evaluate the team member's performance for each of his/her *"Development Actions"* within the Employee Development Profile. Thought Joggers to help you develop specific performance measurements follow:

1. Accuracy *(e.g., percentage of error-free work, reliability of data, confidence level, etc.)*

2. Actual Effectiveness *(versus plan)*

3. Autonomy *(i.e., independence)*

4. Availability

5. Clarity *(or conciseness)*

6. Compliance

7. Consistency

8. Cost

9. Currency *(e.g., how new is the information)*

10. Customer Satisfaction *(client relations, loyalty, etc.)*

11. Dimension *(e.g., verbal, written, on-line, etc.)*

12. Ease Of Reference

13. Employee Satisfaction

14. Follow-Through

15. Frequency

16. Functionality

17. Format

18. Price

19. Quality

20. Quantity

21. Responsiveness

22. Scope

23. Timeliness *(e.g., lead time, response time, down time, cycle time, etc.)*

24. Thoroughness *(or completeness)*

25. Yield *(e.g., profit, return on investment, etc.)*

EVALUATION METHODS

You can't always be there to observe each and every employee behavior. But, you can collect and share facts, figures, and other important information from written sources. Examples follow:

You can also collect and share observations and perceptions from others through interviews, surveys, focus groups, etc. Examples follow:

WRITTEN SOURCES

- activity reports
- business plans
- calendars
- charts and graphs
- *"critical incident"* files
- customer letters
- Employee Development Profiles
- employee self-evaluations
- feedback planners
- Human Resources files and records
- operating manuals and references
- past performance evaluations
- performance plans
- performance standards
- policies and procedures
- position descriptions
- project charts and schedules
- project status reports
- proposals and contracts
- strategic goals, objectives, and tactics
- surveys
- team goals and objectives
- time sheets
- your personal notes

HUMAN RESOURCES

- consultants
- contractors
- internal/external customers (*including department users*)
- internal/external suppliers (*including other employees*)
- past/current supervisors
- peers
- senior managers
- subordinates (*direct reports*)
- team members from around the organization
- witnesses to *"critical incidents"*

UNDERSTANDING WHY EMPLOYEE DEVELOPMENT PROFILES SUCCEED OR FAIL

REASONS FOR SUCCESS

1. The team member is a participant in the development process, rather than just a spectator.

2. Visible, tangible, and/or clearly understood results and expectations stimulate interest and accelerate development.

3. Team members want to see immediate job and personal benefits from their development.

4. Team members want specific, real-life strategies and solutions which will satisfy their needs and interests.

5. Development plans based on past experiences and current knowledge will usually be easier to understand and retain.

6. People remember things they see more readily than what they only hear.

7. Problem-solving methods and materials are more conducive to adult learning.

8. A number of team members working together with common interests can be developed faster than the same people working alone.

9. On-the-job skill development must be used as soon as possible to be retained. What we don't use, we lose!

10. Team members learn more and at a faster pace in a positive, supportive environment. They must be free to express their viewpoints, challenge ideas, share their experiences, and learn from others, without punishment or embarrassment!

REASONS FOR FAILURE

1. The Employee Development Profile is used to solve a problem that is not related to a skill deficiency:

    ✖ Nonperformance is ignored

    ✖ Nonperformance is rewarding

    ✖ Desired performance is punishing

    ✖ Desired performance doesn't matter

    ✖ Desired performance cannot be achieved due to obstacles

2. *"Development Actions"* are not directed at specific *"Areas For Growth;"* there is no particular need for development.

3. *"Development Actions"* and/or *"Expected Results"* are not clearly defined and agreed upon.

4. The team member sees no perceived need or benefit (*i.e., there is no "2.5 Rule" description of an "Area For Growth"*).

5. The team leader is not prepared; they don't want to help, and/or they don't have adequate knowledge of the task or basic employee development principles.

6. The training materials or approach are not relevant to the development goals or to the employees.

7. There is no means for receiving feedback, revising the development process, or evaluating the results.

8. There is no means for reinforcing behavior; recognition, reward, and incentive systems are absent.

LINKING PERFORMANCE EVALUATION AND COMPENSATION

One of the most important uses of performance evaluations in many organizations is that they form the basis for pay systems. While there is no question that *performance* of job responsibilities should be a *major factor* in the decision to grant pay increases, there are a number of challenges associated with using performance-evaluation ratings to directly affect pay increases. Here are only a few:

1. When a salary adjustment is combined with a discussion of performance, often the only thing an employee hears is the salary adjustment. Conduct two separate discussions.

2. In cases of *"salary freezes,"* or limited merit budget funds, it is extremely difficult to appropriately compensate for high performance levels. Apply flexible ranges of salary increases for varying performance levels that coincide with current merit budgets.

3. The market value of a particular job skill may inhibit *(or increase)* the amount of a salary adjustment *(and this may have little connection with performance)*. Clearly differentiate all reasons for changes to compensation *(e.g., merit increase based on performance, salary adjustment based on market changes, cost of living adjustment, etc.)*.

All of these reasons only reinforce the necessity of making performance evaluation an on-going process!

OTHER MAJOR CONSIDERATIONS IN SETTING SALARIES

When it is time to make salary adjustments, several considerations are essential in that salary decision. Therefore, always consult with your Human Resources/Compensation Specialist.

1. Performance of job responsibilities.

2. External equity: Placement within the market salary range for the position based on the Position Description *(job scope)*.

3. Internal equity: Relationship to others' salaries *(e.g., peers, direct reports, management, etc.)* within your organization.

4. Experience: Industry, company, job.

5. Overall value to the organization *(e.g., indispensability, unique skills, knowledge, abilities, experience, etc.)*.

6. Placement within your organization's salary range.

7. Economic state of your business and/or industry.

8. Current wage and salary guidelines *(i.e., merit budget)*.

9. Etc.

AVOIDING COMMON MISTAKES

Some of the most common mistakes team leaders make when they conduct performance evaluations are described below, along with suggestions to help you avoid these mistakes.

COMMON MISTAKE	SOUNDS LIKE
Abdication When team leaders disregard one of their primary responsibilities—developing their employees. These team leaders hire and fire and hire, hoping to score soon.	*"It's not my job to develop people! It's their responsibility. This isn't a school, it's a business. Besides, I don't have the time. If there's a 'weak link,' I simply look for someone else."*
Out-Of-Touch When team leaders do nothing to collect and act on employee performance data, often available from others. Acting like *"victims,"* these team leaders blame others for not doing the team leaders' job.	*"How can I evaluate or develop my people if I don't know how they're doing? Our customers never give me feedback on my employees' performance—they just stop asking for 'poor performers.' By the time I find this out, it's too late."*
Last(ing) Impression When team leaders make a favorable or unfavorable judgment about an employee's total performance based on the employee's performance in the last few months, rather than the entire review period.	*"I still can't get over that lousy presentation she made last month. It not only embarrassed all of us, but I'm still fielding complaints. She really surprised me. She's never done anything less than great work...until now. Well, I'll make sure she never does this again."*
Halo/Pitchfork When team leaders make inappropriate positive or negative generalizations regarding an employee's performance based on one aspect or event.	*"Yeah, I know his organizational skills have gotten us in trouble, and he's still lacking in product knowledge. But he's a great guy and easy to work with. We need more team players like him around here. He deserves to move up in this organization."*
Seniority Rule(s) When team leaders grant higher ratings to employees who have held their jobs longer, or just the opposite.	*"No one gets a rating above a '3' or 'Average' until they've been around for a few years. Can you imagine giving some young buck a '4' of '5'? Next thing you know, he'll be looking for a promotion and start screaming, 'Show me the money!' Bill, on the other hand, has paid his dues over the last 20 years. Everyone likes him, and boy, can he hit a round of golf!"*

Ways To Avoid

You are as effective as the employees who surround you. Help employees identify the skills worth developing for a greater return on investment for all parties. Replacing employees may be more expensive and time consuming than developing them. *(Refer to Chapter Two.)*

Be proactive. Don't wait for others to call or see you. Contact them through interviews, focus groups, surveys, etc. Use technology *(phone, e-mail, fax, voice-mail, etc.)* to keep in contact with your employees' performance. *(Refer to Chapter Three.)*

Discuss and document employee performance throughout the review period. Avoid relying on your memory, or waiting until you receive your organization's evaluation form to begin looking for relevant facts. Look for performance trends as well as significant events. *(Refer to Chapters Three and Four.)*

Document performance in all key areas of the employee's performance plan— Position Descriptions, Performance Objectives, and Performance Action Plans. Highlight areas of strength *and* needed improvement. *(Refer to Chapters Two, Three, and Four.)*

Base performance evaluations on objective data. Reward employees for meeting and exceeding performance expectations, not for just showing up to work. Peak performers may stop *"peaking"* if they're unrecognized or if they know lesser performers are unfairly recognized. And lesser performers who are reinforced will continue to meet your *"low expectations."* *(Refer to Chapter Four.)*

ADHERING TO LEGAL ACCOUNTABILITIES

Following are a few legal accountabilities to adhere to within the United States. Variation will be present in other countries.

LAWS AND GUIDELINES TO KNOW

From a management point of view, the requirements of Equal Employment Opportunity *(EEO)* legislation place the burden of proof on, and demand legal accountability from, your organization for its performance-evaluation process and personnel decisions.

The EEO guidelines support two major criteria used to judge compliance with EEO regulations. If your organization meets these criteria, it is considered to be in compliance.

1. No Adverse Impact

Your organization must demonstrate that its Human Resources policies and practices *(e.g., performance evaluations)* have no adverse impact on any of the groups protected by the law *(e.g., age, race, gender, etc.)*.

2. Validation

Your organization must demonstrate a clear connection between the effectiveness of personnel decision criteria and job success.

How You Are Held Accountable

Your organization can be held fully accountable for how team members are managed. As a consequence, the use of updated performance-evaluation systems to back up decisions has changed from a *"desirable option"* to a *"basic requirement and management responsibility."*

This responsibility extends to nearly all aspects of personnel decision making and policy: hiring/selection, training/ development, promotion/demotion, dismissal/transfer, layoff, short-term hiring, incentive plans and retirement plans!

Today, employees who feel they have been victims of bias or subjective decisions by managers or supervisors may well challenge the decision in court. They often win their case if they can prove that the supervisor's decision was not documented in a consistent and objective performance-evaluation process.

To be truly objective in performance evaluation means that others, who appraise a particular employee's work independently, would reach the same conclusion as you regarding the quality of that work.

The "Easy Way Out" Is Costly!

Why wouldn't performance-evaluation documents support a termination of employment decision, for example? Well, when some managers are faced with the task of writing a performance evaluation, they take the *easy way out!* They write more favorable comments than team members deserve. It is extremely risky to the appraisal writer and your organization.

If the performance-evaluation document does not substantiate the actual reason for the termination, a lawyer may argue:

> You've discriminated against this person! No matter what you now say is the reason for discharge, it says right here in black and white that this person was a good performer for years and years! How is it that they became so bad all of a sudden?

In reality, this happens frequently!

The courts state that performance evaluations used as a basis for dismissal actions must be substantiated by objective documentation. Dismissal actions against employees should be based on either lower ratings (*i.e., critical descriptions of behavior*) on a legitimate evaluation of performance or specific violations of work regulations.

Without systematic performance planning and management, organizations risk—even in situations of unintentional discrimination—losing large amounts of time and money on employee grievance proceedings and lawsuits. In addition, there is a potentially devastating impact, or fallout, on public relations, managerial effectiveness, and employee morale!

PERFORMANCE EVALUATION PREPARATION CHECKLIST

**Consider using the sources below as you collect information
for an upcoming employee performance evaluation.**

❏ 1. Employee's self-evaluation.

 ♦ *Employees can be realistic about their strengths and weaknesses. Weigh the employee's self-assessments against other information.*

❏ 2. Employee performance plan *(i.e., Position Description, Performance Objectives, Performance Action Plans; See **Planning Successful Employee Performance** guidebook.)*

❏ 3. Current list of job assignments/projects.

❏ 4. Observations of current performance.

 ♦ *Complete the Performance Evaluation Thought Jogger.*

 ♦ *Collect Performance Progress Sheet(s) that were completed during the performance period (i.e., your ongoing coaching notes. See **Coaching For Peak Employee Performance** guidebook).*

❏ 5. Strategic business plans *(e.g., visions, missions, core values, strategies, goals, objectives, tactics, etc.).*

❏ 6. Project charts/schedules, activity/progress/status reports, and administrative memos and letters.

 ♦ *These accessible documents may provide consistent detailed records of key employee and team accomplishments, actions, events, and incidents.*

❏ 7. Previous performance evaluations.

 ♦ *Determine if last year's performance expectations were met, and why or why not. Review other information for useful information and patterns. Don't assume accuracy.*

❏ 8. Customer-satisfaction surveys and other forms of feedback.

❏ 9. Human Resources/Personnel files *(e.g., including employment-status changes, letters from internal/external customers, etc.).*

❏ 10. Feedback from others *(e.g., former supervisors, coworkers, contractors, consultants, direct reports, suppliers, and customers).*

 ♦ *Weigh these views against other information. This information is useful if the employee worked a portion of the review period under another supervisor, closely with employees in other departments, etc.*

❏ 11. Changes that may have affected the employee's performance:

 ♦ *Organizational*   ♦ *Relationships with customers, suppliers, etc.*
 ♦ *Staffing*   ♦ *Departmental procedures*
 ♦ *Budget*   ♦ *Employee performance plans*
 ♦ *Schedule*   ♦ *Company policy or business law*
 ♦ *Facility*   ♦ *Critical personal incidents (w/ caution!, e.g.,*
 ♦ *Market/competition*   *"was on approved LOA"*

PERFORMANCE EVALUATION THOUGHT JOGGER

THIS TEAM MEMBER SHOULD:

DO MORE	CONTINUE TO
DO LESS	**LEARN ABOUT**
START	**ASSUME RESPONSIBILITY FOR**
STOP	**OTHER**

GENERAL DESCRIPTIONS ABOUT THIS TEAM MEMBER'S PERFORMANCE:

PLUSES	MINUSES

EMPLOYEE DEVELOPMENT PROFILE

TEAM MEMBER:	TITLE:	ORIGINATED:
TEAM:	TEAM LEADER:	REVISED:

AREA FOR GROWTH (Following "The 2.5 Rule")	DEVELOPMENT ACTIONS	EXPECTED RESULTS
1.	A.	A.
2.	B.	B.
	C.	C.
(.5)	D.	D.

ADDITIONAL RESOURCES
FROM RICHARD CHANG ASSOCIATES, INC.
PUBLICATIONS DIVISION

Available through Richard Chang Associates, Inc. and training and organizational development resource catalogs worldwide.

PRACTICAL GUIDEBOOK COLLECTION

QUALITY IMPROVEMENT SERIES

Continuous Process Improvement

Continuous Improvement Tools Volume 1

Continuous Improvement Tools Volume 2

Step-By-Step Problem Solving

Meetings That Work!

Improving Through Benchmarking

Succeeding As A Self-Managed Team

Satisfying Internal Customers First!

Process Reengineering In Action

Measuring Organizational Improvement Impact

MANAGEMENT SKILLS SERIES

Coaching Through Effective Feedback

Expanding Leadership Impact

Mastering Change Management

On-The-Job Orientation And Training

Re-Creating Teams During Transitions

Planning Successful Employee Performance

Coaching For Peak Employee Performance

Evaluating Employee Performance

Interviewing And Selecting High Performers

HIGH-IMPACT TRAINING SERIES

Creating High-Impact Training

Identifying Targeted Training Needs

Mapping A Winning Training Approach

Producing High-Impact Learning Tools

Applying Successful Training Techniques

Measuring The Impact Of Training

Make Your Training Results Last

WORKPLACE DIVERSITY SERIES

Capitalizing On Workplace Diversity

Successful Staffing In A Diverse Workplace

Team Building For Diverse Work Groups

Communicating In A Diverse Workplace

Tools For Valuing Diversity

HIGH PERFORMANCE TEAM SERIES

Success Through Teamwork

Building A Dynamic Team

Measuring Team Performance

Team Decision-Making Techniques

Guidebooks are also available in fine bookstores.

ADDITIONAL RESOURCES
FROM RICHARD CHANG ASSOCIATES, INC.
PUBLICATIONS DIVISION

PERSONAL GROWTH AND DEVELOPMENT COLLECTION

Managing Your Career in a Changing Workplace

Unlocking Your Career Potential

Marketing Yourself and Your Career

Making Career Transitions

TRAINING PRODUCTS

Step-By-Step Problem Solving ToolKIT™

Meetings That Work! Practical Guidebook ToolPAK™

Continuous Improvement Tools Volume 1 Practical Guidebook ToolPAK™

101 Stupid Things Trainers Do To Sabotage Success

VIDEOTAPES

Mastering Change Management**

Quality: You Don't Have To Be Sick To Get Better*

Achieving Results Through Quality Improvement*

Total Quality: Myths, Methods, Or Miracles**
    Featuring Drs. Ken Blanchard and Richard Chang

Empowering The Quality Effort**
    Featuring Drs. Ken Blanchard and Richard Chang

TOTAL QUALITY VIDEO SERIES AND WORKBOOKS

Building Commitment**

Teaming Up**

Applied Problem Solving**

Self-Directed Evaluation**

* Produced by American Media Inc.   ** Produced by Double Vision Studios

EVALUATION AND FEEDBACK FORM

We need your help to continuously improve the quality of the resources provided through the Richard Chang Associates, Inc., Publications Division. We would greatly appreciate your input and suggestions regarding this particular guidebook, as well as future guidebook interests.

Please photocopy this form before completing it, since other readers may use this guidebook. Thank you in advance for your feedback.

Guidebook Title:_____

1. Overall, how would you rate your *level of satisfaction* with this guidebook? Please circle your response.

   Extremely Dissatisfied   Satisfied   Extremely Satisfied

   1   2   3   4   5

2. What specific *concepts or methods* did you find <u>most</u> helpful?

   _____

   _____

3. What specific *concepts or methods* did you find <u>least</u> helpful?

   _____

   _____

4. As an individual who may purchase additional guidebooks in the future, what *characteristics/features/benefits* are most important to you in making a decision to purchase a guidebook *(or another similar book)*?

   _____

   _____

5. What additional *subject matter/topic areas* would you like to see addressed in future guidebooks?

   _____

   _____

Name *(optional):* _____

Address: _____

C/S/Z: _____   **Phone:** ( )_____

PLEASE FAX YOUR RESPONSES TO: (714) 727-7007
OR MAIL YOUR RESPONSE TO: RICHARD CHANG ASSOCIATES, INC.
15265 ALTON PARKWAY, SUITE 300, IRVINE, CA 92618
OR CALL US AT: (800) 756-8096